BAG OF TRICKS

Mixed Stories of Life as a San Francisco Punk
in the early 80's

Book one of a punk trilogy

by Ruby Dee Philippa

Published by Earth Island Books
Pickforde Lodge
Pickforde Lane
Ticehurst
East Sussex
TN5 7BN

www.earthislandbooks.com

First published by Earth Island Books 2025

Cover photos by Annabelle Port

ISBN 9781916864528 paperback
ISBN 9781916864535 ebook

Printed and bound by Solopress, Southend

Dedication

This goes out to all of you who lived any of this crazy punk rock life, who did some of these wild things to ourselves and to one another, who survived or didn't- we had some insane times and we had some fun. Most of all, this goes out to Annabelle. You are so deeply loved and so profoundly missed..

Author's Note

For those of you who never stepped foot inside the punk rock world of the late 1970's to early 1980's, this collection of short stories might hold some surprises for you. Sure, there were off-the-beaten path experiences and great music and all sorts of crazy shenanigans, but there was a darker side to that way of life too. A lot of the punk rockers I knew were estranged from their families of origin, often lived on the streets, and turned to heavy drinking and drugging along with all the other trappings of being a punk rocker.

For those of you who did live that life, please be aware that some of the stories you read here may be disturbing in their stark descriptions of drug use. I wrote it like I remembered it and didn't pull any punches. So if you think you might be triggered by any of what this collection of stories offers, please partner up with a reading buddy, or make sure you have someone lined up as support you can turn to as needed.

It's my intent to bring this part of my history- and that of many others- to light; not to shock or harm anyone in any way. My cohorts from the time and I have kept in touch over the years, and eventually some of the story-swapping we shared in our reminiscences led to my penning these tales. In our conversations, we all agreed that there is a need for these stories to be told. Hopefully you enjoy reading them as much as I did writing them. Please stay safe in all ways while doing so.

Contents

Acknowledgement

I send heartfelt thanks to everyone who shared those crazy years with me. We created and added to one another's stories all along. Without you, none of this would have been written at all. Annabelle, Barry, Paul, Urban, Animal, Annie, Marco, Jenny, Steve, Patrick, other Paul, and more- those of you still with us, well done. And those of you who aren't, we remember you in so many ways. I also have to thank Jorge for putting up with my leave-me-alone-I'm-writing time. You're no angel, but you are one of the best. Most of all, I must acknowledge that while we seemed to be pitted against the world back then, we unwittingly found a community that has lasted through the years. Thank you for sticking around and seeing this life through.

BAG OF TRICKS

Mixed Stories of Life as a San Francisco Punk
in the early 80's

Book one of a punk trilogy

by Ruby Dee Philippa

"It's an odd thing, but anyone who disappears
is said to be seen in San Francisco.
It must be a delightful city and possess
all the attractions of the next world."
– **Oscar Wilde, The Picture of Dorian Gray**

Cold and Fast

1

Fog hits the streets like a magnet to steel. It's stuck and it's sticking hard. On a dark and early morning, citizens sleep sweetly, or not, in their city beds. Three fluorescent orange vests drift from one side of the street to the other, pushing brooms and bending to sweep up what they gather every six feet or so. At the end of each block, they deposit a neat pile of white plastic bags, tied off half full of leaves, paper, and plastic trash.

The vests adorn three young women in their late teens and early twenties. The girls' heads are shaved, and wet from the fog. Moisture runs down their hairless heads and mingles with the sweat on their faces and necks. It stings their eyes. They sing as they work.

"Fuck! Me while you still can! Put! That thing in my no man's land! Babe! You wield that dildo fine! Mom! I'm gonna make you mine!" The girls dance and stomp heavy laced-up boots as they make their way down the street. Their black-rimmed eyes squeeze shut against the fog, the sweat and the act of emoting while they sing.

All three girls wear black hooded sweatshirts underneath their work vests. The sweatshirts are dirty and ripe with age and grease. One of the girls has a tattoo that starts behind her left ear and runs down her neck towards her clavicle. The tattoo is a dragon, breathing down her sweaty neck. The other girls have tattoos too, but you can't see them just now. One has a butterfly speared helplessly on a pin over her right shoulder blade, and the other has a horseshoe nailed onto her left bicep, dripping tattoo blood down her arm.

The girls cackle between bursts of song. They are so pleased with themselves, that they are singing and having such a grand time of it all, even though they are sweeping debris before six o'clock in the morning. A window shade goes up, the window slamming open with a sudden crack above them. A dark figure leans out of the foggy backlit morning window and hollers, "Hey! Shut the hell up! People are trying to sleep here!"

Three sets of middle fingers shoot up into the air at once. It is a well-rehearsed maneuver, and the fingers do it oh so well. Dragon tattoo shouts back, "Fuck YOU!" The girls move away from the building so they can get a better look at their aggressor. They peer up at the window, holding their middle fingers out in salute. The figure grunts "Humph" and moves back inside, yanking the window down in retreat. The girls thrust their fingers in unison again towards the window and drop their hands, shuffling away. They turn and look over their shoulders, yelling out various phrases.

"Fuck YOU!"
"We work for the CITY!"
"You can't tell us what to do, ya fucking HIPPIE!"

The last receives a giggle and nods of approval from the other two. They move to the opposite side of the street and onto the curb. Speared butterfly sits down, stretching her long torn black jeans-clad legs out in front of her. She reaches into the pocket of her hoodie and pulls out a crumpled pack of Old Golds, mouthing one from the pack. She offers the pack around, and the others happily oblige. Horseshoe hands the slim crumpled pack back to her friend and offers her a pack of matches in kind. The girls light their cigarettes, expertly cupping the cigs as they pull smoke into their lungs. Dragon tattoo looks back towards the closed window and narrowing her eyes, spits into the gutter.

"Motherfucking asshole. What the fuck does *he* know?"

Speared butterfly exhales a thin stream of smoke and says, "It was a she."

"Whatever. What the fuck does SHE know? Yeah, I just wear this orange vest and sweep up HER shit for fun! All she had to do was LOOK and see that we're working. For the city. For HER. Christ! Fucking hippies. Sometimes I hate the Haight."

Dragon's friends pull at their cigarettes, waiting for what comes next. Dragon tongues a piece of tobacco off her upper teeth and spits it into the street. The girls stand or sit and look around them, up at the buildings and sky, which has begun to pale towards daylight. A thin sheen of pearly light seeps between the buildings to the east. The girls can see one another's eyes without the heavy arc of a buzzing streetlight above them. Sophie, with her dragon tattoo, throws her cigarette down and crushes it with the heel of her boot. She stands and looks down the street, then back at her friends.

"Shit, well we should finish up before traffic starts. Only two more blocks. Come on."

The other two shuffle forward and mumble something about white slavery. But the city job pays for beer and rent when they owe it. It's a cushy situation, as they can dress how they want, work with friends, and not really have to answer to anyone while they work. The city has provided these jobs as a part of one of their programs to move the plethora of grungy city street kids off the streets and into paying jobs and housing. Other options, aside from sweeping streets in the early morning hours, includes working at the health clinic or other various social service outlets the city has set up in odd neighborhoods throughout San Francisco. The girls prefer to sweep the streets, as they don't have to dress up or talk nicely if they don't feel up to it.

They grab hold of their brooms and bags, and hastily push together a pile of wet dirt and trash over which they've been standing and sitting. Val, the speared butterfly, bends down and holds a wide, rusty, bent metal tray for the other two to sweep trash onto. They sweep the dirt up, and Val empties the tray into a nearly empty bag. They move down the street more quietly, buzzing from their cigarette break, each intently thinking about quitting time just up ahead.

Val waits for her friends to create another pile of trash for her. She walks ahead, leans against the building down at the end of the street, and bending one knee, braces her foot against the acid-crumbling façade of the wall. The other two work in unison, a choreographed ballet with brooms.

Val turns to look into the window of the ice cream shop against which she is leaning and thinks how tasty an ice cream sounds right about now.

"Hey guys, let's go to Petrini's and grab some ice cream on our way home!"

Amy, the bleeding horseshoe, looks up and smiles out one side of her mouth. She grew up on a farm in Ontario and learned that smile from her favorite older brother. Anything he did was too cool for school in her mind, so she did it too. Now it is her signature smile.

Sophie yells back, "Nah, I can't. Man, we better not show up without any beer! I only got enough cash for some suds, and Henry wanted a beef stick too." Her voice cracks, as it always does, icy gravel in the way she talks. She stops sweeping and looks to Amy. "Whatchya think, sweetcheeks?"

Amy grins and ducks her head. She is easily shaken, and not much used to attention, even from her own friends. She pushes her broom a few strokes further along, then looks over at Val.

"I have a few bucks, Val. I need to get some cigs anyway. I owe Sophie, like, half a pack."

Val does a little jig, pirouettes up onto the toes of her steel-hulled boots and curtsies. "Well, let's get fuckin' finished up then! I don't want to be late like last week!"

Sophie snarls back, "If you didn't smoke all my cigarettes, we wouldn't be outta time! Besides, as long as we finish up by the time traffic gets going, what the fuck do they care?"

A softly puttering car swings past them around the corner and down Haight. Val smirks, "See?"

Sophie snarls again, "What the fuck...?" She takes issue with being told what to do and when to do it, and the end of their workday always riles her up. She attacks the leaves in front of her with her broom and hurries to catch up with Amy, who is already down at the end of the street, waiting for her with Val. Sophie catches up and slaps Amy joyfully on the back. Another day, another few dollars in the pocket.

The girls shoulder their brooms and dustpan like soldiers bearing arms and march off up the street towards the panhandle, where the city van should be waiting for them. Val and Amy hunch slightly: angular, thin and underfed. Sophie has more heft and curves, yet still manages to carry herself in that lanky, loping manner the other two manage effortlessly.

Tiny pebbles scrunch beneath their boots as they scuffle along, Val humming the song they'd sung earlier. Thin as they are, all three girls walk with a swagger- some serious street attitude. They are proud to hold these jobs. They are the only ones in their set of friends and acquaintances who work for The City, unless you count Pete's mom, Pat.

But she had her injury over a year ago and has been sucking off city compensation ever since. She spends it all on coke and her Rasta boyfriends, the ones who come to stay for a few days and then leave. They spend most of the year touring or living with their families in Jamaica, so Pat has many lined up, one after the other, to keep her satisfied until the next one comes to town. And meanwhile, she can always rely on her pal, Coca.

Sophie walks a few steps ahead of the other girls. She is the leader of this little group, though no-one ever says as much. She wants to get home and climb into her bed with Henry before he gets rolling for the day.

Henry moved in between her sheets a few weeks ago, and that means a lot to Sophie. She's always wanted a little piece of that man. Smiling to herself, she thinks of his leather and beer smell, how it fills the sheets and books along the shelf behind her bed. He smells like a skinhead should: masculine and slightly sweaty.

Sophie picks up her pace and glances back at Amy. Amy had been with Henry before, though she doesn't seem to mind the change of arrangements. She's a sweet girl, and never wants to shake things up. Besides, there's this one dude who just moved to town that has Amy perked up again. That always helps heal a busted, if not broken, heart.

The city van is just ahead, parked up on the curb in the corner yellow zone. The cab light is on, though it's now light enough to read the headlines in the newspaper boxes the girls walk past. No-one reads the headlines. They just don't care. They head for the van, straightening up and removing their orange city worker vests. A slight, dark woman sits in the driver's seat, blowing spit-rimmed pale pink bubbles and reading a Steven King novel. As the girls first tap on the passenger window and then open the side cargo door, she marks her place with a gum wrapper and looks up.

2

"You're late ladies. You shoulda been here about 30 minutes ago." She raises one eyebrow and looks at Sophie. She always talks to Sophie first. Sophie always answers.

Sophie purses her lips. "Yeah, some guy or lady, I don't know which, got in a tizzy that we were making too much noise. We weren't, I swear. They argued with us out their window, telling us to go away. Made us lose some time. Sorry about that. We had to go real slow and work quieter, like mice or something."

The driver looks unimpressed. "Welp, whatever. Just know that I have to mark that down. You don't get overtime, either way. And if there's any complaints, you know... Try to work quieter, alright? Go ahead and throw your things in the van. Do you need a ride home?"

Sometimes, the city driver gives the girls a ride home if it's raining. Today it's fine and clear, as the fog lifts. The girls look at each other and shake their heads no. Shrugging off the feeling of the vests and work, they move away from the van. Val raises a hand in farewell, and Amy follows suit. "Seeya." They move off furtively, as if they'd just handled a drug deal, and cross into the park.

Cutting past the evenly spaced eucalyptus trees, Amy inhales deeply of their sharp oily scent. The three trip along, avoiding dog shit and spent hypodermic needles, and make their way across the narrow strip of park to the opposite street. They jaywalk. Sophie does cartwheels on the sidewalk, but something sticks to her hands, so she stops, wiping her palms on her also-dirty jeans.

"Fuckin' street cleaners not doing their jobs." She grins and moves to catch up with the other two. They link arms and walk together in sync, moving first left legs, then right, sweeping each leg out and to the left or right in unison. They call this 'doing the monkey'.

They arrive at Petrini's Market and cross over to the Salvation Army trailer parked near the trash bins at the end of the parking lot. They jump into the enormous pile of abandoned items left as donations, picking through mounds of damp clothes, mildewy books, boxes of household goods, and furniture. They chuckle over saggy underwear, enormous bras, small crusty kid's sweaters, torn fancy stockings, ripped jeans, old hippie hip huggers, and t-shirts of all shapes, colors and sizes. The girls grimace "Ewwwww…" and throw the hip-huggers against the side of the truck. Who knows what hippie germs those pants and things could carry?

Amy finds a small silvery chrome piano-shaped jewelry box. She opens it and 'Edelweiss' tinkles out from its worn fuzzy red felt interior. She runs her fingers along its hard-cast keys, and smiles. She loves this song. The case goes into her hoodie pocket and she turns to the boxes of books behind them.

Sophie picks up a stretched out dirty white corset. It has buckles and things that hang down. Sophie has no idea what goes where, but she loves the idea of it all. "Hey! Maybe we can sell this and... look, there's some others... to the girls down the street! What's their names?" She looks over to Val. Val remembers names and things that aren't so important to Sophie.

"You mean Mouse? Annie-X?"

Sophie snorts. Annie-X lives a few doors up from the girls, but even she is too large to squeeze into this oversized corset. Annie-X models herself after Marilyn Monroe, bleaching her hair and styling it, doing her makeup like Marilyn. But Annie-X weighs about two hundred and fifty pounds, and she carries a baseball bat.

She is a huge, two hundred and fifty pound baseball bat-wielding Marilyn. Annie-X sells speed and hand paints leather jackets and armbands for other punks. She rides her Alva skateboard up and down the streets of San Francisco, pouting and making eyes like Marilyn, scaring everyone with her bat. "Mouse, yeah. Her and all her dancer friends. Maybe they can do a show around it."

Sophie refers to another neighbor, a gorgeous long-legged girl who pays her way in the world by dancing at one or another of the Mitchell Brothers strip clubs. She is famous for her specialty dances, and for teaming up with other girls to perform crafted dance stories for her regular clients.

"Or Larry!" chimes in Amy softly. She smiles shyly at the other two, and they burst out laughing. Larry lives somewhere unknown and is a fucking fag. He loves to wear women's clothing, especially costumes with a theater affect to them. Val thinks, 'Larry may be a fag, but he's all right too'. He drinks a lot of hooch and is always good for a swig at shows. Besides, he's entertaining.

The girls paw through the rest of the donations. A few early morning customers drift past them with disapproving looks on their faces. The girls ignore them, turning their heads away in bemused distraction. Sophie empties out a paper bag filled with hairpins and broken, headless Barbie dolls. The girls drop in handfuls of corsets and a couple of t-shirts. Amy lets out a whoop.

"Whal, lookie here!" She holds out a moist, floppy oversized paperback. On the cover is a bad color photo of a turkey, close-up and slightly out of focus. "No way. This is frigging GREAT. Look!" She holds the book out so both the others can see the title and cover photo more closely. "It's a book on how to kill turkeys! THIS should go on the coffee table. If we had one."

Sophie reaches for the book. "Shit. That is perfect!" They all grin at one another. They feel young and clever and oh so cool. Not like the poor slobs rushing past them on their way to pick up lattes and piss off to whatever brainless jobs they hold out there. The girls love being together, on this wavelength, and just outside society's 'normie' boundaries.

Val rolls the paper bag under one arm and the girls climb off the pile of tailings they've left behind as rejects. They walk through the double doors that silently slush open as the girls enter the market, leading them into a world of bright light and tinkly supermarket background noise.

A Muzak version of Michael Jackson's 'Thriller' is piped in around them, and the girls do a slight shuffle, raising their arms zombie-style, down the aisle.

If any of the girls had hair, they would all be blonde. They all have blue eyes, and Amy's are the deepest blue of them all. People stop her on the street and often ask her if she's wearing contact lenses to achieve that color. She ducks at the attention and whispers 'no'. Embarrassed by any sort of scrutiny, Amy is subject to it oftener than not. She is the most striking and naturally beautiful of the three.

She tags along behind Val towards the ice cream aisle, while Sophie splits off from the trio to grab Henry's beer. As Amy and Val pass the end of the frozen foods aisle, Amy reaches into the display case that just happens to be open there, snagging a carton of Old Gold's. By the time the two reach the ice cream, the cigarettes have disappeared, nestled safely against Amy's thin chest. She hunches her shoulders further and thrusts her hips forward slightly to keep the cigarettes from slipping out from under her shirt.

Val pauses a moment in front of the cold frosted doors. She cups her right elbow with her left hand and pulls at her lips, stroking and gently lifting them together with the fingers of her right hand. This is a big decision. The calf on her left leg itches now, so she stands on that foot and rubs the top of her heavy boot against the back of her leg. She has a new tattoo there, a small pile of steaming turds with the inscription 'The Shits' beneath it, written in cholo street-style lettering. The Shits is the name of the band Henry is in, and the girls all love them. They attend every show The Shits play in town, and even accompany them to nearby road trip shows whenever possible.

Val opens the cold glass door and reaches in for a short carton of Haagen Daz caramel. She changes her mind and lets the door bang shut. Cold frosty air escapes and the glass fogs up, blocking her view. Val re-opens the door and just stands there, chewing her lower lip. Finally, she reaches in and grabs a larger carton of strawberries-n-cream. She holds it up for Amy to see, allowing the door to shut behind her.

"This ok, Doucie?" Doucie is Val's pet name for Amy. It's what her grandfather had called her when she was little, before he died and left her alone with her mom and her often-distant papa. Val hails from northern Quebec, and since Amy is a Canuck too, Val talks to her in French. They often mix French and English together, and sometimes revert to French only when it suits them to talk about someone right there who doesn't understand.

The problem is that Amy understands French but doesn't speak it all that well, so Val does most of the talking, and Amy says 'oueh, d'accord,' every so often, in agreement. Sophie sometimes tries to follow along with her high school French, but eventually ends up quitting and turning away.

Amy nods her head up and down in agreement. She usually enjoys what the others enjoy, and strawberries and cream sound perfect right about now. That, and a shot of something cold and fast. Maybe afterwards. For now, Amy is happy they're getting ice cream, cigarettes and beer, then heading home. She thinks maybe she'll bake some cookies later today too. She loves to bake, shoot speed, and skate like a demon up and down the Panhandle. And hang out with her friends, even if they do tease her too often at times.

Val starts to walk up the aisle and Amy follows, looking for Sophie. With a quick glance down the empty beer aisle, they re-route towards the check-out stands, where they hear Sophie's broken glass voice.

"What the fuck?" Sophie snarls. Her lip curls back. She is royally pissed off. She forgot her fake ID and is arguing with the early morning manager. Val walks quickly towards their friend, while Amy, conscious of the cigarette carton digging into her tender breasts, hangs back.

Sophie turns to her friends. "If we don't bring beer home, Henry is gonna shit. For real." What she's thinking is that Henry will think she's a waste of time, a real wipeout. And she doesn't want that at all. She appeals to Val, "Tell him, will you?" Her pretty, wide smooth face furrows into a knot of tension and she picks nervously at the ragged wrists of her hoodie.

She adds, turning back to the manager, "I always buy beer here. So I forgot my fucking ID this morning. Hey buddy, I just got off work- we all did- and I'd really like to go home and have a fucking beer! The kind of work we do... I don't always carry my ID with me."

Val and Amy both nod in agreement. The manager looks tired. He looks like he really doesn't want this. A small crowd of local business-type folks have turned away from the coffee stand at the front of the store and watch to see what will happen next.

The manager looks at the clump of well-dressed customers and then back to the three punks in front of him. To tell you the truth, he wants to say, I could use a beer too. He's been at work all night, and now has to stay and cover for the jerk who called in sick. Another fucking double, another fucking day. And now this... He raises his arms, and his shoulders shift too. "There's nothing I can do, ladies. Why don't you go home, get your ID, and come back? I'm happy to hold this up front for you and sell you your beer then."

That gets Sophie really ticked. "THAT'S. NOT. The PLAN. ASSHOLE. I would like to buy my beer BEFORE I get home from work. So I can drink it when I get there. See?"

The manager tightens his lips. His eyes narrow slightly, with a gleam of 'right back at ya' in them. "There is no need to use that sort of language. I can hear you very well without it." He looks around for support. The two checkers busy themselves with details on their registers, though no-one is checking through them right now. The small crowd holds its breath and looks around suddenly- nothing happening here- waiting to see what Sophie will do next.

A middle-aged man in a tie-dye t-shirt walks past Amy. He is listening in but trying to mind his own business. His old lady sent him up to the store, and all he wants is to get what she sent him there for and get back home. Val notices him and follows him down the bread aisle. "Hey mister. Do you have any ID on you? Our friend forgot hers, and this dude won't let us buy any beer."

The man scratches his head and reaches for one of his messy, sprung dreadlocks. Val thinks, 'fucking hippie,' but doesn't say it. She smiles instead, and the hippie smiles back.

"Don't you think it's too early to be drinking?"

Val coughs. "Yeah, but not for us. We work for the city, and just got off work. Besides, not too early for a bong hit, huh?" The hippie reeks of weed, smoke and incense. Val scores a direct hit. The hippie shakes his head, tossing his nasty dreadlocks from side to side. He stops and looks Val in the eyes. "Right. Nope. Hah. Yeah, I can buy your beer. Whatchya got?"

Val holds one arm out in a gesture that says 'right this way,' and walks with the hippie over to where Sophie and the manager still stand off, silently waiting for someone to do something. Val takes the beer off the counter and hands it to the hippie. She raises a finger to the manager and says, "This guy's gonna buy it. We don't need you anymore."

The girls laugh and follow the hippie over to the next checkout stand. Sophie lifts her shoulders back, and turns her head, eyes flashing defiantly, to watch the manager standing alone as they walk away. He looks like he's about to say something, then he exhales a short burst of air and stands down with a slight military bearing, defeated.

He turns to the crowd of latte sippers and says "Good morning folks! Thanks for coming to Petrini's! Is there anything I can do for anyone?"

Some smile, some shake their heads 'no', and everyone turns away, leaving the poor man alone. He throws his shoulders back and marches to the back of the store, where the icy plastic flaps billow gently from the cold air of the temperature-controlled storeroom. He is definitely going to have that drink now.

The hippie buys the girls their beer, and Val offers him one as they walk outside. He says no and turns around and walks back into the store. What was it his old lady wanted? Damnit...

Outside again, in full clear daylight, the girls grin at one another. What an adventure! Sophie hugs the Black Label in its crisp paper bag to her chest, pulls out a handful of Beefstix from her hoodie pocket, and flashes them at the other two.

Amy looks around, then steps away from the door, motioning her friends to follow. She lifts her hoodie and a corner of her raggedy t-shirt beneath to show them the bottom of the Old Gold's carton there. She slides the cigarettes from beneath her shirt, and Val and Sophie let out a whoop in unison.

"C'est bien fait, ca!!!!!" cries Val, and she hugs Amy in a sideways pal-hug. They laugh and walk quickly into the parking lot and towards the street, towards home.

3

Val carries the ice cream and the crumpled bag of corsets and the turkey book. She's ready for a beer now. NOW, she thinks.

They pass the end of the market and dance into the street. Turning the corner, they walk the block it takes to bring them to the apartment where they live together. A gray-haired, filmy-eyed black man leans against the building next to the front door of their place. He is drunk already, or maybe he hasn't been to bed anywhere yet, but he doesn't see them either way. His rumpled button-down shirt is miss-buttoned and crusted with something- vomit, urine, a spilled drink- and doesn't offer enough protection on such a chilly Fall morning.

But the man is so inebriated, or so far gone on something, he doesn't quite notice just how cold he is.

The girls carefully step past him and Sophie sneers. He is one more reason the girls shave their heads. All their friends do. The Shits, and others. They shave their heads to show a public sense of unity, together for certain things, and against others. And one of the things they are against is blacks. They don't like Orientals, Mescins, hippies, or yuppies, but they most of all hate niggers. The niggers and hippies live all around them and are clearly the more urgent problem at hand. If you stay out of Chinatown or The Mission, you can avoid most of those others, but the niggers and hippies are everywhere.

Once past the drunk, Sophie turns and spits on him, leaving a large, gooey gob of spittle hanging like a pearl from his arm. He doesn't even notice. Amy stops and looks back at him as Sophie heads up the stairs. She doesn't hate him. She twists thoughtfully at the silver cross hanging from one ear. She'd been thinking of trying to find a swastika to hang there instead. There are so many death rocker chicks all over San Francisco wearing crosses in their ears, almost like a badge to some not-so-secret society. But Amy'd received the cross, as part of a pair of earrings, on her last birthday home. That was a long time ago. That was last year. And actually, she's not sure she really *wants* to wear a swastika. She doesn't hate anyone, really. She just likes doing what her friends do.

She looks up the stairwell, then back down at the man. Tiptoeing back down the stairs, she breaks open the carton of Old Gold's and hands the man a pack. His fingers close around the cigarettes, and he tries to smile, his lips splitting apart from their unbroken, sealed-dry crust. He really wants a drink, but he'll take the cigarettes, thank you...

Amy rushes back up the stairs in time to catch the door as Val lets go of it. She reaches inside the doorway and flicks on the hall light, wishing Sophie wouldn't stomp around so loudly, so early. She gently closes the door behind her and leans against it, thinking what to do next.

Down the hall, in the kitchen, Val puts the ice cream into the freezer. It's time for a beer, after all that excitement. She kicks at the overflowing bags of trash that spill out next to the filthy fridge and onto the stained linoleum floor. No one has mopped this kitchen for a very long time. Plus, it's the end of the month and they missed their trash day. Again.

Sophie stomps back into the kitchen from the bathroom where she'd splashed water onto her pits. She picks up a few stray wax paper candy wrappers and tucks them into one of the trash bags.

Val sits on the lone broken chrome and Naugahyde kitchen chair to loosen the laces on her boots a little. She's not ready to take them off, not on this filthy floor, but oh the relief...

Amy pushes herself away from the door and moves past the other two into the smallish room just off the kitchen, near the back porch door. She sleeps alone there now, but not for long, if she has it her way. She emerges in a fresh t-shirt, just as greasy as the last, but dry and with a lesser stench. She's slapped some cologne on too, her favorite, that an old flame used to wear. Every time she puts on a little, or when she waves the bottle past her nose for the scent, she can see him. He was a soccer player back home in Ontario, on exchange from South Africa, and he'd been so gorgeous. Long legged, sandy blond hair cut like Sting's 'do, and oh those blue-green eyes, like glass...

Amy licks her lips and crosses over to the fridge. "Beer?" She opens the sticky fridge door and reaches in. She grabs one, two, three beers, and carries them over to the rickety kitchen table. It used to be someone's dining table, though it lost its dining appeal long ago. Made from now-grey wood and set on shaky lathe-turned legs, it suffers from a variety of knife-gouges and graffiti carved into nearly every surface. Splinters rise up and catch sleeves and wrists. The girls had rescued the table from the Petrini's Market Salvation Army trailer when it was in better shape. But now, it's fallen prey to their lifestyle and is deteriorating further every day.

Amy hands Val and Sophie a beer apiece and leans against the wall. Sophie cracks hers open with a loud pop and gurgles that first long, satisfying swig of the cheap, yellow suds. She raises the can in a toast, turns, and heads up to the front of the apartment. Softly, she opens the door to the room she now shares with Henry. Looking in, Sophie feels a touch of awe. There he is, humped under a pile of dirty sheets and worn-thin blankets. His back is turned to the doorway, yet she can still see his chest expand into his ribs as he breathes deeply in and out. She quietly enters the room and shuts the door behind her. Placing her beer on the floor, she sits on the edge of the mattress and peers over at his face, still in shadow from the morning light.

She looks up at the shelf above her bed, decorated now with Henry's collection of dead things. A flattened crow, a desiccated cat they'd found beneath the back porch stairs, the skull from Pat's old Tom, Ziggy, cleaned to a soft white china sheen. Sophie adjusts her position on the edge of the bed, and watches Henry sleep. She feels so satisfied. She feels safe, like he's hers, or she's his, when he's asleep. She doesn't have to share him with anyone. Not Amy, not Max or Gabe- the other members of the Shits- and not with any of his adoring little mealy girl fans who hop to whenever he's around.

Just thinking of who she doesn't need to share him with brings her down a little. She looks out the window, then back at Henry, and sighs. She leans over his body and watches his eyelids flutter against the soft daylight and whatever dreams he's dreaming. Oh what a beautiful man. He has cheekbones that run for miles. Sophie reaches back for her beer and after taking a sip, rolls the perspiring can across Henry's forehead. Henry slaps at her hands.

"What the fuh...?" He opens his eyes. "Jesus, Sophie. What did I tell you? Don't fucking wake me up like that. I hate surprises. What if I hurt you?" Henry spent four years in the Army, stationed in Germany. Sometimes, he likes to show off maneuvers. Sometimes he hurts people, by mistake. Especially if he's been drinking, he forgets to hold back, and someone gets slammed down too hard, or a bad twist in their arm or neck. Sophie is sometimes that someone, and most of the time, it doesn't matter so much.

"Well, I guess you don't want any beer then." She smiles coyly at him and holds the beer away from his reach. She turns and takes a drink, looking down at him aslant over her cheek. Henry sits up and grabs her waist. He pulls her closer to him and buries his mouth into her neck. Her hoodie gets in the way and she sloshes the beer. Sophie grins. She puts the beer down on the shelf, next to her two vintage Oz books, and wraps her hands, fingers interlaced, behind his neck. Leaning in, they suckle on one another like that for a few minutes.

A loud crash from the other room separates them. They both look towards the door. Sophie growls, the taste of

Henry hot on her lips. "What the fuck are they doing now? Christ, I swear, it's like we have a couple of kids sometimes." She widens her eyes and looks at Henry, frightened suddenly he'll take that the wrong way. He does, but smiles and shrugs, no harm, no foul. Sophie hands him the beer and wriggles out of his grasp. She walks to the door, throws it open, and yells, "Keep it DOWN out there! There are people trying to FUCK in here!" She slams the door shut.

The kitchen erupts into guffaws and giggles, then shhhh, quiets down. Sophie has her hoodie and shirt off by the time she has reached the bed again. Henry reaches for her, fingers splayed in greedy want. He touches the tip of his nose to the scar that starts just above Sophie's navel, wraps around it and travels south into the shadow of her jeans. It is an old playground scar, from a frightening fall off the slide and onto the low fence that surrounded the sandbox at Sophie's kindergarten school.

Henry loves the scar. He licks the thin, puckered line around her belly button and down, down... Sophie struggles to stay on her knees in front of him, but he pulls her into him and rolls over so that he is now lying on top of her. The sheets are twisted and dam up between them. Henry catches at the thin gritty material with the toes of both feet and yanks the sheets down. And there they are, the two of them, chest to chest, ahhh...

In the kitchen, everyone rolls their eyes at the squealing and moans that come from the front bedroom. Max has joined the two girls, walking in half-awake, scratching the fleabites that cover his stomach and calves. Max's room has fleas, but somehow they haven't reached the rest of the house.

Max stumbles into the dingy kitchen and sits on the broken-down orange nubby couch that rests in the corner by the stove. The couch is moldy and spattered with grease, tomato soup, and grains of rice and macaroni. Stuffing spills out from its skunked arms and flat, misshapen cushions. It sits on the floor, having lost all four legs years before anyone can remember. The couch was here already when the girls moved into the rooms they rent from Pat.

When Max sits on the couch, his legs double up and point his knees up towards his ears. He grabs his prized skateboard that was resting against the arm of the couch and spins it, upright on one end, on the floor. The skateboard and his drum kit are his two favorite things. He loves to skate, and equally loves to drum. Anything that gives him that controlled rush of power, of hard hitting, bashing, and sweaty, intense flight. Speed does the trick too, but drumming and skating are free- more or less- once you have the gear, so they win out.

Amy narrows her eyes at the spinning board. Max places it

on the floor and rolls it back and forth with both feet placed side by side on its deck. Amy and Max have had an on again, off again flirtation for a long time now, even while she was messing around with Henry. Amy thinks it's mostly because they have so much in common. They both love to skate, and skate hard. Yet they're both afraid to make a move and start things up.

Max sees how other dudes watch Amy. He watches them move in, and he stands back and hangs with her, her skate buddy. Amy just wavers and lets things happen to her, no matter what she really wants to have happen next.

Everyone teases them about it. "When are you two gonna finalize this and make it official?" Comments like that. They ignore the remarks pointedly, jump on their decks, and skate off. Neither one will start this thing up. Neither one seems willing to risk losing what they already have.

Max sniffles and wipes the back of his hand across his nose. He drinks the beer Val just handed him. He is just now waking up, much too early for how late he was up last night, and really wants some coffee, but a beer will do.

"It's too early man... you dudettes work way too fuckin' early..." His voice drifts off and he takes another gulp from his beer.

Max was born and raised in Berkeley. So were Henry and Gabe. They all went to the same high school and surfed off the California coast whenever weather permitted. Now they talk and sound like a badly written surf movie script with a little German gestalt thrown in for good measure.

Max doesn't surf anymore, ever since his punk friends began to make fun of his cottony sun-bleached hair and called him Beach Boy. He shaved his head, pierced his ear, got a couple of tattoos, and quit surfing.

But he misses it. Every Sunday, he and Amy and a bunch of other tough skaters run the length of Golden Gate Park to the beach. They visit the buffalo, put on faces and pose for the tourists and families picnicking along the way, and stop for calzones and eggplant parmigiana on the Upper Aves, often panhandling for their fare. Once at the beach, Max gazes longingly at the breakers, wishing he had his board, and that it wasn't so uncool to surf. He'd be there right now if he could be.

Instead, he picks at the stickers mounted on the topside of his board. ALVA, FANG, FEAR, they say. Beneath those, a handmade claw-mark sticker runs from the top to the base of the deck. Max rests one scabby hand on the uncapped nose of the board and finishes his beer.

"BRRAAAP." Max thumps his chest. "Ok... any more?" He stands and walks over to the fridge. Looking back at Amy, then Val quizzically, he opens the door and takes out another Black Label. "Hey... is there anything to eat?"

Finally having removed her boots and soaked socks, Val perches on the rickety chair and picks the stale, moist fuzz from between her toes. She looks up and jerks her chin towards the front of the house. "Beef stix, in the chamber of love. That's about it. Unless you find some crackers or something up there somewhere." She nods at the filthy cupboards above Max's head.

Max moans and sits down on the couch again, head hanging down between his shoulders. "Well shit-fire." He looks up. Ok, so who wants to go to the soup kitchen with me? Is it even open today?"

Val turns her mouth down, nope. "Naah, but hey, *that* shouldn't take too long." She jerks her thumb towards the front of the house and grins. Val looks over at Amy and breaks into an even bigger toothy smile. Amy's told Val how quick to the draw Henry is. Something to do with all the drugs he takes. Amy blushes and stands, sliding herself up with her back pressed against the wall. She compresses her lips together slightly and shakes her head 'no, don't go there' in a plea to Val. She walks over to the window looking out over the back porch and beyond that, the yard.

The window is filthy though, and Amy can barely see through the dirt-streaked glass. She cups her hand over her eyes and tries to peer through the heavy streaks, both inside and out on the windowpane. She thinks about the farm back home. Right about now, her mom would be cracking eggs and frying up a pound of their home-cured bacon. There would be home-baked bread too. Amy gets her love of baking from her mom.

Farm equipment scares her though, so years ago, she decided to make her way off the farm and into the city for school. She'd applied to study International Political Science at a number of colleges across Canada and the States and had been accepted at SFU. She'd also been accepted closer to home, but the thought of jumping the border and living this strong, solitary life deep in study, pouring over tomes of wisdom, had appealed to her more than remaining closer to home. So she accepted her scholarship and SFU entrance, and moved to California.

Her brother Robert drove her across the plains and mountains of the Northern US, a place she'd never been before. As they neared San Francisco, she began to have doubts, but Robert guessed at her fears, and relieved them.

"You'll be FINE." He said. "Mama-n-daddy didn't raise no dummy. You're here on scholarship, right? That counts for a LOT." He shook his head. Amy explained that she wasn't afraid of failing in school. She knew she was smart that way. She was afraid of all the people she'd have to meet and deal with. Strangers, every one of them. And being so far from him, her big brother...

He understood. "Ok then, what's to prevent you from coming home if you need to? Or having me come out? As long as it's not harvest. Well hell, even then." He gave her that sideways smile.

They'd pulled into the City, so enormous and alien. As they drove through the city streets to her dorm near campus, Amy peered in awe at the people, the rain, the tall buildings, and once they headed north past the downtown area, row after row of houses, stretching as far as she could see. She reminded herself she'd come here to escape a future life shackled to the stove, the gestation pens and slaughterhouse, and the baby machine she was be expected to become.

A few weeks after unpacking her two boxes of books, hanging the rainbow curtain she'd brought from home over the single small window, and registering for all her classes, she'd ventured out into the City. And met Henry on the bus.

She'd climbed onto the number twenty-eight bus on Holloway and settled into her window seat, watching the condensation roll past her as the bus picked up speed. It was raining outside, and the inside of the bus steamed, smelling of wet wool and rubber. Amy avoided looking other passengers in the eye, dreamily allowing her eyes to gaze, unfocused, at the drenched city outside.

She changed buses at Lincoln and 19th, heading towards the Haight, a place she'd heard so much about. Henry had been waiting for the number seventy-one there, and allowing her to board first, followed right behind her. The bus was only half full, but Henry, having just come home from Germany, wanted something new in his life, something attached to the City. He followed Amy to her seat and sat across the aisle from her. He kept trying to catch her eye, this hot little blonde with the little bangs of fringe across her eyes. But she avoided his looks, and determinedly stared out her window.

Finally, he leaned over and asked, "Hey, uh... is this the right bus to Haight Ashbury?"

Amy looked up, inverted her lips between her teeth, and shrugged. "I hope so. I called Muni info and was told to catch this bus. I'm, um, not from here."

Henry lifted his chest. "Well I am. And yeah, I'm pretty sure this is it. Thanks." He looked up the aisle of the bus and back at Amy, smiling, "Where ya from?"

They talked the rest of the bus ride and got off at the end of Golden Gate Park, where Henry pointed out landmarks, and gave Amy her own private tour of the Haight district. He took his seaman's cap off over coffee, and Amy couldn't help but ask about his shaved head. That led to an invitation to come hear The Shits play that night in the Mission, and the rest became history. Amy met new friends, eventually shaved her own head, and dropped out of school, though she still considers it time off from studies for the time being.

Every so often, as now, Amy thinks she would like to take her friends back to Ontario and show them the farm. She imagines their faces when they see the two-story farmhouse, the sturdy barn, and all the cows and pigs. The boy-men would charm her mother, saying 'please' and 'thank you ma'am'- words they don't often use here in The City- asking for seconds and more of Amy's mom's famous apple pie. They would try to get a rise out of the docile cows and have fun feeding the pigs. They would eventually become as bored as Amy had been.

But her mom doesn't know she's shaved her head. They

don't even know yet that she's taking the year off from school, though it's been nearly ten months already, and she hasn't made any moves to go back. It's just that there's no way she's going home now, either. Not yet, not yet, not yet. Amy shakes her head 'no' and turns back to face the kitchen.

"What about that ice cream?"

Val smirks and opens the freezer. She pulls out the brand-new carton hesitantly, thinking how she'd changed her mind. She's decided to do a shot of speed first, maybe get some painting done, and *then* settle down with a bowl of ice cream. But, she sighs to herself, Amy gets what Amy wants... She places the ice cream on the counter next to the sink with a thunk and waves her hands at the pile of dirty dishes.

"Go ahead and find yourself a bowl or something. I'm not serving!"

4

Val walks out of the kitchen and down the hall to her room next to Sophie's, carefully picking her way barefoot across the crusty, sticky debris and leaves her boots outside her bedroom door. She turns back before entering her room. "Leave some for me!"

Amy squeaks back a reply, "We will!" And Val slides into her room, ready for that first shot of the day.

Shutting the door behind her with a satisfying click, Val snaps on the small porcelain lamp perched on the crate next to her bed. She wipes the sole of each foot against her pants legs, and heads straight for her dresser, against the wall opposite the doorway.

Her papa had made the dresser for her years before. Her mom had painted it baby blue, and Val has yet to paint over it, though she hates the color. It was one of the few things she brought with her when she moved to The City. She doesn't mind losing anything else, but this one thing, she clings to protectively. This and a few photos are all she has of her papa and mom, it's been so long since they've talked. On top of the dresser, she's arranged an assortment of knick-knacks, found items, and photos, and on display in the center of everything, her kit. Val unfurls the thin leather roll to expose its inner pockets, holding a neat, bent-just-so spoon, a straw, a razor, a tiny bevel-edged mirror, and orange-capped rig. Slipping her fingers into the unsnapped pocket along the top edge of the soft reddish-brown leather, she removes a small bit of folded cellophane: a nearly-full quarter of sparkly white crystals.

Val runs a fingernail along the edge of the tape holding the cellophane shut, unfolds the packet, and taps a nickel's worth into the spoon, which she's placed on the dresser next to her kit. She uncaps the needle, holds it up to the light coming into her room from the window to check for any dents in the needle itself, and dips it into the glass of water she always replaces daily, by the kit's side. So what if it gets a little dusty, it's never hurt her before.

Next, she pulls back on the plunger, sucking 5cc's of water into the needle's chamber, and adds that to the bowl of the spoon. Using the tip of the needle, she stirs her concoction and licks her lips. Then she holds the rig in one hand and pinches a tiny piece of cotton from a ball tucked in next to the straw with her other. She rolls that between her finger and thumb and drops it into the spoon atop the cloudy speed mixture.

Her eyes moisten in anticipation. This is the best part. Lowering the tip of the needle into the mixed speed slush and against the soaked cotton ball, Val pulls back on the plunger again, slowly and steadily. She holds the needle upright and taps any residual air bubbles away. Placing the needle between her front teeth, she slips the multi-colored Indian scarf from the top dresser drawer knob around her right arm, pulls it into a tight loop, and trades the needle for the scarf's end between her teeth.

She taps at the vein in the crook of her right arm, raising it slightly. Placing the needle against her flesh there, she pushes the tip into her vein gently, and pulls back once again on the plunger, releasing a heavenly, drifting cloud of blood into the needle's chamber. She pushes the plunger all the way in, slowly, deliciously, and releases the scarf from her teeth simultaneously. She coughs, a tiny forced exhalation that explodes from the back of her throat. Oh, ca c'est bon.

Val hangs the scarf back over the drawer knob, rinses her rig in the glass of water, and puts everything away in reverse order. She licks the spoon and wipes it against her shirt, and chews on the fragment of cotton like a piece of gum.

After rolling her kit back up and straightening her collection of things on the dresser top, touching them more than moving anything around, Val turns to her closet, and the paints and canvases she has stashed there. The light is good, she decides, and the mood is right. She loves when her plans come together like this. She can get high, paint an hour or two, and when she's ready to come down, there's beer in the fridge, and most of a pint of Jack Daniel's hidden in her sock drawer. She lets the painting begin.

Amy and Max, meanwhile, are making their way through the pint of strawberries-n-cream. They take big bites that hurt their teeth, then suck on the spoons until the freeze in their brains dies down. Amy is quiet, even quieter than usual. Today is payday, or maybe it's tomorrow, she can't remember. It's been almost a week since she's had any speed, and she wants to score, take a nap, then get up, shoot up, and hit the park for a satisfying ride. She doesn't know about Val's stash. Val keeps her drugs close to the chest like that, and no-one ever knows.

Amy wanders from the kitchen back into her room and lays down on her unmade bed. It smells like Henry's dog, Buster. Buster hasn't got used to the fact that Henry sleeps at the front of the apartment now, not here any longer, off the kitchen. He must be out back just now, tethered to the base of the porch one story below them.

Amy stretches her legs, arching her back and allowing her

body to go rigid, then fall lax against the crumpled sheets. She holds her legs straight up into the air above her, and notices how bow-legged she is, even in this position. She rode horses for years, even dabbling in a little Gymkhana, and her legs just won't seem to straighten out. She rolls over, and facing the wall against which her bed is butted up, picks at the wallpaper there. She rolls a tiny piece of it back and forth and tugs at it, pulling a long thin strip of dust-scented beige paper away from the wall. She sighs.

Looking up at the tour posters taped to the wall above her- The Dils, The Avengers, The Dead Boys, The Germs- Amy thinks about home again. She knows she has to tell everyone about dropping out of school. They've been pestering her for news about her grades. She can't keep lying to them for much longer. She's never lied to them like this before, and she feels terrible about it. Especially about her brother. She's always told him *everything*, and now she doesn't know how to start.

Max tosses the empty carton of ice cream at one of the trash bags. It bounces off the pile of debris and spatters a few droplets of melted sugary cream onto the floor. He jumps up, picks the dented carton off the floor, spins around, and dunks it hard into the least-packed bag.

"Score!"

He looks over at the door to Amy's room. She's left it open, but somehow it doesn't seem like an invitation to join her there. Max walks over to the sink and begins drumming on whatever is closest at hand. He picks up a pair of spoons and whacks them against the counter, the pile of fat-rimmed plates in the sink, a scummy-soaped frying pan, and the cabinet doors. He rat-a-tat-tats a nice little drum roll on the edge of the sink and finishes with a percussive smack against the table behind him. He's trying to get Amy's attention. Maybe she'll go for a skate with him. They can panhandle and pick up some burgers downtown.

Amy doesn't notice though. She's started to doze, drifting off to dreamy images of her old bedroom back home.

Sophie and Henry have finished their business, chugged back the rest of the Black Label Sophie'd brought with her, and fallen asleep at opposite edges of the bed. Sophie throws off a lot of heat in her sleep, and Henry sweats. So they move as far away from one another as they can and still be in the same bed together. Sophie snores slightly, little troughs of air channeling their way out of her once-broken nose.

Val is sucking on the wooden tip of her paintbrush. She stands back a little from the canvas propped against the back of a wooden chair in her room and ponders what to do next. She's painted the outline of a gnarled old oak tree, and a pair of Cheshire cat eyes gazing back at her. She's unnerved by the eyes. She thinks they're watching her, and if she moves, they follow her around the room. She turns away from the canvas, aware that she's turning her back on the eyes.

Val looks out the window, squinting against the bright light. Her own eyes feel tired. They hurt in the dazzling daylight, and she decides she's done painting for the day. She lays her palette down on the edge of the chair next to the canvas and tosses her brushes into the glass of water on the dresser. She scoots the tubes of paint scattered around her on the floor together with her bare feet, and sits on the edge of her bed.

Now what? She knows the other girls are asleep. She can hear Sophie snoring from the next room. And the fact that Max is drumming and not talking with Amy tells her that Amy has passed out too. Val thinks, 'well, merde...' and gets up again. She opens her sock drawer and pulls out the slender bottle of JD. "Here's to the end of another great day," she says to herself, and takes a long, hot swallow of the cool liquor.

She sits back onto the edge of her mattress and drinks, waiting for something to happen next.

Belize: Hell or heaven?
[Roy indicates "Heaven" through a glance]
Belize: Like San Francisco.
— Tony Kushner, Angels in America

Tough Like Marilyn

1

Annie removes the short cigarette stub from her much-loved vintage brass holder and places a fresh, new, jasmine-scented cigarette in its proper place. She lights the new cigarette off the old butt and takes a sweet, long drag at it. Oh, that's nice. The brass is cold between her teeth. She tosses the stubbed-out butt towards the bottom of the stoop and enjoys her morning smoke. Chomping at the cold metal bit, she rolls her tongue over the mouthpiece, imagining herself a Hollywood starlet.

Annie adjusts her buttocks on the chilly cement stairs. She spent all last night carousing the clubs and skating tough from North Beach to the Haight, and she's just stepped from a short, hot shower into a 1940's vintage cream-colored quilted robe- the one with the poker hand stitched across the collar and the bell-shaped pocket that's just the right size to hold her cigarettes. Her shoulder-length bleached hair is tied up in a red hankie, pins holding various curls in place.

She releases a thin, cool, sweet stream of smoke and leans forward, wrapping her arms around her ample legs. Though quilted, the robe is thin, and her butt cheeks are turning to stone. She thinks she'll find herself some sort of cushion to absorb the chill out here and allow her to sit like the lady she imagines herself to be, in high style.

Annie looks down the street towards the Clits' house. The Clits are a small knot of chick Shits lovers, and most of them have banged the guys in the band, so they're really sort of all one big happy family. Annie likes the oldest, Sophie, for her caustic attitude and sexy, rough voice. The other two, she could take or leave. Amy-something-or-other is from some hick farm out in the middle of Canada somewhere, and Val is pretty uppity with her inclination to speak French when she doesn't want others to understand what she's saying. Other than that, she'd be all right. Amy is a skater too, so that makes her more worth Annie's time. But still, the whole hick thing grates.

Sometimes, the Clits stop by Annie's after their weekly work shift for the City. She sells them speed, and they bring her gifts lifted from the Salvation Army donation trailer around the corner. Some days they shoot up at her pad, then spend the morning chatting about upcoming shows, gossiping, and cooing over Annie's roommate's pet albino rat. Annie plays records and dances with them like Marilyn would, in seductive, coy poses around the room.

Every now and then, she shows off a newly purchased or traded piece of Marilyn-ana: her favorite is the chipped black marble ashtray with a miniature carved Marilyn seated in a pin-up pose along its edge. Other adored pieces are her silver-framed photo of Marilyn and Joe at some function- Marilyn looking fresh and lovely in a calf-length tweed skirt and matching jacket trimmed in fur- and her brand-new Marilyn Playboy nudie picture-printed sheets.

Annie models herself after her idol. She bleaches her hair to a nearly white blonde and curls it into that classic Monroe-do. She purses her cherry-painted lips, and lines her eyes with Marilyn's signature makeup style. At shows, she poses, and affects a wispy, soft Marilyn voice.

Then she skates off, tough, like she *knows* Marilyn would have, if only she'd had a skateboard instead of all those pills. If she'd been a punk, she'd have been all right. Annie shares this theory with anyone who will listen, and that's pretty much everyone, as she sells the cleanest speed around the City these days.

Annie-X hails from Los Angeles. She moved to San

Francisco in pursuit of a man. Once she got there, she decided he wasn't worth it and began fucking women instead. Her first girlfriend told her she looked a little like Marilyn Monroe, and that's when her obsession started.

Annie is an institution in the City now. She skates hard and can be seen at every show selling her wares, leaning against the wall in a come-hither pose. She weighs about two hundred and fifty pounds, but that doesn't stop her from modeling herself after Marilyn. Annie carries a battered hickory baseball bat and will gleefully beat anyone who mocks her idol in any way.

As the day brightens, the steps begin to warm slightly too, but Annie's butt cheeks are numb by now, so she figures she'll move the party inside and make herself a nice nightcap of instant hot apple cider in one of her new Marilyn mugs. She tilts her head back and takes one last, long drag off the cold, floral cigarette. She hears a 'ting!' and feels a sudden sting in her neck.

Annie touches her neck with her free hand, and feeling something wet, holds that hand up to see what that might be. Her fingers are tipped in blood, and she gasps and fumbles her cigarette holder before looking up and down the street. There is no one out there, not even a car driving by. It is still early, though late enough that all the morning commuters have already hiked off to their bus stops or driven away an hour or so ago.

Annie stands up, and holding her free hand to her neck again, tosses the burning cigarette away and slips the brass holder into her robe pocket. She opens the door she'd left ajar and runs up the stairs to her second-floor apartment. As her feet hit the first steps, she hears another 'ting!' behind her. Without pausing, she barrels up the stairs and into the bathroom. She gasps again, "What the FUCK?"

A small bright red oval nests on one side of her neck, a few inches from her Adam's apple. Annie presses a towel to the light trickle of blood, and notices a tiny bump on the other side of her neck, mirrored opposite where the first hole throbs. She touches it and feels a solid lump.

"Oh shit. That's... What the hell?" She decides to go to the Haight Clinic to check this out. Squinting at her reflection, she's pretty certain there's something lodged in her neck that doesn't belong there.

Annie walks quickly into the dining area where her bedroom is set up. Keeping one hand on the towel pressed against her neck, she wriggles her way out of the robe and digs through the pile of clean laundry on her bed. She pulls out a pair of elastic-waisted soft cotton pants with a pattern of razors printed in red on one leg and black on the other, and a Dead Kennedys t-shirt, and gets dressed. Tucking the ends of the towel underneath her t against her neck like a fighter, she straightens her do-rag, throws her leopard print cat-eye shades on, and hurries over to the door.

She grabs her wallet and keys and slips on her black pom-pom topped bamboo mules at the top of the stairs. Mules flapping against the soles of her feet, she runs downstairs and out the door. As she hurries down the street, she wishes she saw someone she knew so she could ask them to come with her to the clinic. She is scared, but she can't show it.

As Annie runs across the Panhandle, she realizes she forgot her skateboard and she grimaces to herself. She could have been there by now. She passes a few early morning Haight types: a scraggly hippie in tie-dye, a couple of fags in coral and turquoise button-down shirts sipping lattes, a stray dog, sniffing at someone else's pee. She huffs past them all and doesn't say a word.

She rounds the corner from Cole onto Haight, then up the street to the free clinic. What luck! Their doors are open. She realizes she had no idea whether they were open this early or not. Frowning, Annie realizes she has no idea what time it is. She pushes open the door and skids to a stop in front of the tall counter.

"Hello? Hey! Hello! Can someone help me? I'm bleeding! Hello!!" Annie leans across the counter, and the Formica wood groans. She hears a clinking sound from somewhere in back and calls out again. "HEY! I need some HELP out here!"

A ruddy-cheeked blonde steps out from a storage closet behind the counter area. "Hello? Yes, what can I do for you?"

Annie leans forward again and waves the fingers of her hand holding the towel in place. "I... I'm bleeding. I'm not sure what happened, but I think I've got something in my neck and I'm bleeding." She pulls the edge of the towel down to show the blonde.

"Did you swallow something?" The smile disappears from her cheery face and is replaced with a look of appropriate concern. Annie sighs.

"No. I was sitting out in front of my place, on the front stairs, and I felt this sharp sting. I mean, I wasn't doing anything, just sitting there. Then this sting, and blood started coming out of this hole. See?" She tilts her head to one side and shows blondie the hole.

The receptionist frowns. "Oh geez. Ok, let me get you in to see the doctor right away." She raises both arms and waves Annie around the counter to a small exam room down the hall. Guiding Annie into the room, she says, "The doctor will be here in a sec, ok?" and she scurries off.

Annie leans on the strip of sheer white paper centered down the length of the table and looks around. She's been here for paps before, but not anything like this. She hopes they can help her figure out what the hell happened and fix it. Annie knows they have facilities here for crazy stuff like heart attacks and detox, she has friends who've come here for both.

Little Deb from Detroit had been freebasing coke and her heart went into some sort of freakout. They helped her with that. And loads of Annie's street buddies have tried to kick heroin here, or at least come for the freebies they hand out as a go-between high during dry spells. Annie can't really respect that. As far as she is concerned, you either quit or earn the money you need to keep going. It's the way she's always done it, and what she expects of everyone around her. Pansy-asses grubbing off the City for free highs. Huh.

Annie looks up as the receptionist ushers the doctor into the room and shuts the door behind him. Annie thinks he looks just like someone playing a doctor on TV with his gray hair, tiny chin dimple, and loose white smock over chinos and scuffed brown loafers. She feels relieved.

The doctor holds both hands out. "Sandy told me you're

bleeding from your neck. May I see?" He asks firmly.

Annie pushes the edge of the towel away from her neck for him. She tries to see if anything leaked onto her shirt, but her ample breast and belly straining against the 'Dead Kennedys' and 'Too Drunk To Fuck' seem unbloodied.

The doctor peers closely at Annie's neck, lightly touching his latex-gloved fingers near the edge of the hole. Annie turns her head slightly. "There's this too." She points at the teeny lump on the other side of her neck. The doctor says, "Hmm", then turns and opens a drawer, searches for something, and removes a small hooked instrument. He turns to Annie's neck again and prods lightly at the lump with the tip of the instrument. Annie winces, thinking it might hurt, but it doesn't.

Blood has stopped trickling from the hole on the other side of Annie's neck, but now it's starting to sting, like road rash. Just as she is about to say something about the pain, the doctor turns again, soaks a fresh piece of gauze with alcohol, and places it lightly on the wound. "Hold this, will you?" he asks. Annie touches the gauze gingerly with three fingers and holds it in place. Oo, that's cold!

The doctor cleans the hooked instrument and says, "This might sting a little, but hold on and let me know, ok?"

Annie grunts, "This other side is starting to hurt. Really, it stings like a son of a bitch." She shakes her head, "I'm fine. Go for it."

The doctor looks up briefly into Annie's eyes, then back down at her neck. He places the tip of the instrument against the lump and moves the hook up and down, forward, back, up again. Suddenly Annie feels something shift and catch. The doctor rotates his wrist and sluices the intruder out of a second tiny hole in her neck into the palm of his other hand. He raises his hand so she can see. It is a tiny black ball, shiny and slick with her blood, and not at all what Annie imagined.

She scrunches her brow into a look of concern. "What is it? A Rock?" She can't figure this out. What the hell happened?

The doctor presses his lips together slightly to one side of his mouth. "Actually, I'd say this is a BB shot." He pauses and looks Annie cautiously in the eyes. "Were you playing around with a gun with someone?"

Annie's eyes go big and round. "No! What the...? I swear. I was just... sitting on my front steps, having a smoke. Then I heard this 'bing!' That's all that happened. I felt a harsh sorta sting and went and looked at it and saw the one hole. I- I didn't see the other hole. This one was bleeding, so I ran over here. I *swear.*" She frowns at the doc. What the hell. A BB?

"Hmm. Ok. Then we need to call the police." The doctor shows her the BB again for emphasis.

"The police? I didn't DO anything!" Annie doesn't like the cops. In her line of business, you learn to avoid them. She thinks, do I have any speed in my wallet? She searches the wallet in her mind and comes up empty, so it's probably ok. Still, she doesn't like dealing with the cops.

"No, no. I didn't think so. Listen, have you heard of the Haight Sniper?" He leans back over the counter behind him, plucks a kidney-shaped pink plastic tray from a stack against the wall, and drops the BB into it. It lands with a small wet clink.

Annie nods. "Well, yeah. Didn't he kill a couple of people a few weeks ago?" She pulls at the gauze against her neck slightly, but it sticks, pulling her skin. "Ouch."

The doctor takes the dirty gauze, cleans her neck lightly, and places a fresh bandage on the wound. He steps on the footpad of the white cylindrical trashcan near the door, popping its top open, and drops the gauze in as he says, "Yes. Actually, he's killed four people in the last few months. If this is the same person, you are one incredibly lucky lady. Let me have Sandy call the police. You just wait right here. Do you need anything? Some water? I'll get that for you."

Annie shakes her head, no. She watches the doctor remove his gloves and drop them into the trash as well, then open the door and step into the hall. "Sandy!" He calls out, and quickly walks away.

2

Annie closes her eyes. What the fuck? Did she really get *shot*? Then she smiles to herself. This is something to show and tell at shows for a while. Hot *damn*! And there's no reason to exaggerate the details. Hmm... what would Marilyn do in this situation? She kicks her legs out as she ponders. Well, first off, she would want something to dull the pain. GodDAMN it's starting to hurt.

The doctor walks back in. "Ok, the next step is, we need to drain this. I'm going to run a piece of gauze tubing through the area where the BB went through. It won't look pretty, but it will prevent any infection from setting up shop. Ok?" He hurries over to the shelves and drawers and busies himself with pulling out more instruments: needles, thread, more gauze, little packets of ointment.

Annie pauses. Not pretty? "Uh, hey doc? Is there any other way? I'd rather not have a scar..."

The doctor lays out his tools as he answers, "Actually, by doing this, we'll reduce the size of the scar considerably. And there's the risk of infection to consider. I don't think I'm going to allow you any choice in this matter." He turns and looks at Annie. "But I misspoke. We're not *leaving* the gauze in place. I'm going to run the gauze through the path the BB took, flush it, then remove it. Then after a week, as the wound closes up, I will need you to come back in so we can look at it to make sure it's healing properly. Hmmm?"

She nods, ok. As long as she can get something for the pain. And she's so tired now. She's been up all night and is starting to come down from all this excitement. There's a buzzing sound coming from somewhere in the clinic she hadn't noticed before. It makes Annie feel like they're inside of some 1950's outer space alien movie. She can smell coffee over the scent of antiseptic and alcohol, and it comforts her. She sighs and settles in to allow the doctor whatever he needs to do.

He dons a new pair of latex gloves from the box marked 'L' on the counter. Then he unrolls a small, narrow flat piece of gauze from its' plastic case, cuts a length, and attaches it to a thin plastic needle. Annie tries to get a closer look. The doctor pats a bit of alcoholic ointment onto a cotton swab and dabs at the holes on both sides of her neck. Annie holds the piece of wet gauze away from her neck while he does this, and crumples it between her fingers against the cold, hard steel of the table, in expectation of how this is going to hurt.

The doctor presses the tip of the plastic needle into the opening of the larger hole, and wriggling it, pulls it slightly to the right, across her neck. No wait, that's *inside* her neck! Annie freezes a little in shock. She can feel a funny sort of tickle and burning across the inside of her neck. She wants to scratch it away but grasps the cold table with both hands instead. She coughs.

"Doc? Are you almost done?"

He pauses. "Does this hurt? Maybe itch a little? I'll give you some ointment for that. I've run a gauze tube through the route of the projectile through your neck. And now..." He pulls his hand away from her neck, unthreading the gauze from the second smaller hole. Annie peers in awe at the stringy bloody gauze as he tosses it into the can along with his gloves.

The doctor washes his hands and as he tapes fresh bandages onto each side of her neck, says, "As the holes close up, you'll need to make sure to keep them clean. You may have small scars but those should fade in time. It will probably itch like crazy, so I ask that you refrain from scratching. Use the ointment, here..." He gestures towards a small pile of square white packets on the counter, "And you should be fine. I'd like to see you in a week to see how you're doing then, ok?"

"Ok, so... this is like stitches?" Annie wants to touch the

bandages but is afraid she'll scar her neck. She reaches up and pats at her do-rag, making sure it is still keeping her hair in place.

"Exactly. Here. Take a look. Because we cleaned the path the BB took, it shouldn't become infected. The openings will completely heal. Just try not to pick at them as they do." The doctor hands Annie a hand mirror from one of the drawers. She holds it up and looks. Ewww... She smiles at herself. She's got a little of that Frankenstein thing going on now. Very cool. And her kerchief is still where it ought to be- her hair looks great.

"Ok. And the scars will fade, you think?" She holds the mirror to one side and then the other, going back and forth to see more easily from side to side. She can't help but notice how pretty she looks with her hair up like that, holes in her neck or whatever.

The doctor nods, and clasps his hands together in front of him, just like a doctor on TV. Funny about that. Annie likes this guy, even if he *is* straight-edged. His hands have a light brush of silver hair across the knuckles. They make him seem dignified and for real.

"Yes. I do. Now let's get you set up with another appointment for the end of the week. You can wait for the police out front in the waiting area, then you go home and get some rest. Here, take these." He hands her the small pile of ointment packets.

"Um, doc? Can I get something for the pain?" Annie bats her eyes slowly, once. The doctor leans back against the counter and crosses his arms.

"Are you *really* in pain? Or just a little discomfort?"

Annie smiles softly, opening her lips just so. "Oh no. I'm not in a *lot* of pain. But it *does* hurt a little. I mean, I'm not asking for Dilaudid or Demerol... just, I don't know. Do you have anything *light* that will help?" She lowers her chin slightly and gazes up at the doc.

The doctor lets out a sigh. "Yes, I can prescribe you some Tylenol. I don't want you taking anything stronger, as A, I don't think you need it, and B, I don't want to thin your blood at all. You need to allow this to clot naturally." He uncrosses his arms and turns to rifle through one of the drawers behind him.

"Here we go. Take two of these, no more than once every eight hours." He hands Annie four small red and white printed square packets. She piles them on top of the others and drops them all into one of her pants pockets.

"Thanks, doc." She bats her eyelashes once again, making sure he knows how grateful she is. Tylenol, my ass, she thinks.

Annie drops down off the table, trying not to jar her neck. Will she be able to skate with this thing? Yeah, she figures. She can skate drunk, high, shot, whatever. She follows the doctor out into the hall and over to the counter area. Sandy is looking through a calendar on her desk, writing various things with colored pencils in the little day squares. She puts the pencils down and stands up. "How are you? The police should be here any second."

The doctor nods, "That's fine Sandy. Let's get Miss...?"

"Annie," purred Annie, keeping to her Marilyn persona.

"Miss Annie, let's get her set with a check-up next week. I'd like to see how she's doing."

Sandy looks down at the calendar. "How long? Half hour ok?"

The doctor nods. "Yes, fine. You take care, Miss Annie, and I'll see you next week." And to Sandy he nods again, "Let me know if the police need anything from me. Here's the BB." He hands Sandy a small glycerin packet with the BB nestled inside. Annie reaches for it, then drops her hands. Right, the cops will want that.

The doctor reaches for Annie's hand in return and shakes it. "You make sure to call us or come back if anything seems strange. There might be some slight drainage, and that's normal. But if they bleed again or become swollen or red, let us know." He releases Annie's hand and places it on her shoulder. "You'll be alright. Just make sure to take it easy for a few days and see what happens, alright?"

Annie shrugs softly and turns her face to one side. "Sure thing, doc. Take it easy, don't scratch it. Got it." She looks over at Sandy. "Can I get a cup of coffee while we're waiting on the cops?"

The doctor raises his free hand in farewell, drops the other hand from Annie's shoulder, and turns down the hall. Sandy smiles, "Sure! Wait right here. Do you need any cream or sugar?" She shrugs and points to the small closet. "All we have is creamer packets; that dry stuff, you know?"

Annie loves those packets. She grabs a handful whenever she goes to IHOP and snacks on them, just pouring the powder right into her mouth. It's like a dry milky version of instant Jello. "Oh that's fine. If you don't mind, bring me a few extras just in case I need more 'cream'." She holds her hands up and makes air quotation marks. Ooh, why did she do that? She hates when people do that. She *must* be tired, for real.

Sandy hurries into the small closet again, clinks some dishes and glassware around, and comes out with an oversized mug of coffee and three packets of creamer. The mug is pale mauve, and has dancing deer, or are those moose, on it? Annie can't tell. They're singing 'Tra La La' and dancing. Looks pretty wussy to her but whatever. She takes the offered mug and pockets the packets of creamer. Her pockets are bulging now. Annie wishes she had a jacket or backpack of some kind. She hates not looking her best.

Glad there's no one here after all to see her looking so rumpled, Annie looks around. Well, she might as well sit and wait. There's no one in the waiting area, so she has her choice of where to go. She saunters over to the window next to the front door, peeks out, and strolls past the couch and table there. There are folks walking along the sidewalk outside, but no one Annie recognizes. She walks over to the wall adjacent to the front window, where a large framed collection of snapshots hangs. She studies the snapshots, and smirks. Most of them are of hippies at some outdoor show or other, covered in dust and dreadlocks, receiving treatment for dehydration or LSD freak-outs, she figures. But hey! She knows *that* guy! Annie rests one knee on the wicker chair and leans in. That's Andrew! He's a buddy of hers from around The City. Annie thinks he's from Sacramento or around there. He's a redheaded Tasmanian devil and breaks little punkette hearts left and right. He and Annie sometimes compare notes about their women. They hold up the wall together at the Mab, discussing technique and who they're doing now.

Annie scans the great patchwork of photos and sees a few other faces she knows, but none that well. She coughs and touches one of the bandages on her neck. Man, this better not leave a huge scar. She turns and sits on the wicker chair beneath the photomontage, and sips at her coffee. She pushes her lower lip out. Hmm, not bad, Sandy.

The police walk through the door a few minutes later, ask questions, and take Annie's statement. She crosses her ankles and smiles her great Marilyn half-moon smile. Neither of them seems to notice her obvious charms. Annie places both hands on the insides of her thighs and leans forward, pressing her breasts slightly out and up. How about *them* apples, Misters? *Now* they seem to take notice. They smile at her, and tsk when she says how hard it's going to be for her.

Eventually, they have all they need, including the small cellophane packet holding the BB. One of the cops, the one most likely to admire The Village People, Annie thinks, holds up the packet before placing it in his chest pocket. "Whew. This looks like the Sniper. You are one *hell* of a lucky gal."

Annie smiles mischievously, "That's what I keep getting told. We'll see how lucky I *really* am." She winks at the cop. He chuckles and turns to the door, where his partner waits for him to finish up.

"Yeah, well, yes ma'am. Thanks for all the information. And you take care." He bumps into his partner in his rush to get outside. Annie snorts, thinking, 'nice feel!', and finishes her coffee.

"Ok, thanks Sandy. Here's your cup. I can go now, right?" She places the mug on the counter. Two street urchins walked in while the police were there, interrogating Annie. They sat down on the couch farthest from where Annie and the police were talking, watching curiously to see if they could figure what she'd done. She spins around and vents at them now, "HEY! Anything you'd like to ASK?"

Remembering her persona, she gathers herself and poses coyly. "I'm happy to tell you anything you'd like to hear."

The two kids sit there mutely, straggly clothes and all.

They're part of the recent army that has been hitting the streets lately. Homeless, running away from everywhere and everyone, looking for something or someone to replace what they maybe never had. Annie feels for them but can't be bothered too much. They're not customers, and there are so many, she can't place any faces or names. There was one kid who got picked up at the Soup Kitchen a few months earlier. Sweet kid, but somehow, her folks found out where she was and came and took her home. She squalled and fought, but the cops made her go with them. Annie wonders if that's how it will end for most of this new crop.

A lot of her friends are cast-offs, runaways, escaped from broken homes. But they're all older now, old enough to be on their own, or at least, their families don't care enough to send the police after them. Annie loves her knot of friends, those she does business with, those she skates with, those she goes to shows with, and those she 'does'. Well, she wouldn't call them friends, exactly, more like little chickens. And she's the hawk. But she sure does like all that tender meat...!

She lunges forward on one leg at the two kids still sitting there meekly and raises her arms into a Mexican wrestling pose. "AARRGH!" Then, oh shit! That hurt. She stops, touches both sides of her neck gingerly, concerned, and presses her lips together. She looks over at Sandy, who is concentrating on her calendar again.

"Ok well. I'm going now." Making sure she has her wallet and keys, Annie scrunches up her neck towel in one hand and jingles the door open to the bright day outside. Looking back, she notices with satisfaction the two kids leaning in towards one another and whispering. Ok, they were cool. They didn't scare when she tried to spook them, and *that's* tough, like Marilyn would be. *Now* they can talk.

Annie steps firmly onto the sidewalk and places both hands on her hips. What a night. A looong night. Now she's ready for that apple cider. And some home fries! And bacon! God is she hungry. Can she eat bacon or will eating solid food her neck? She decides to head down to her favorite greasy spoon at Church Street Station and take a chance. Fuck, she doesn't have her board. And she's not walking that far in these little heels. Well? She pirouettes on the sidewalk and nearly runs into Larry, who breaks into a grin.

"Lady Monroe!" He opens both his arms to her, then notices the small bandages adorning her neck. "What *happened*?"

Annie sniffs the air around Larry before giving in to his hug. He often doesn't wash for days, and she can't stand that sweet, decaying sweat-encrusted smell that clings to the air around him. He smells pretty clean today, even a little like... what is that? Green apple? Hmmm. Ok. She steps in for his embrace.

"You'll *never* believe this: I got shot."

Larry pushes her back abruptly, holding onto her shoulders. "What...? You got SHOT?" By who? When? Where?"

Annie laughs and holds up a hand to stay Larry's questions. "Woah! Take me to breakfast and I'll tell you all about it."

Larry pauses and licks his lips. He looks nervously around Annie down the street. "Well... I'm not hungry. But, ok. I *am* thirsty. Can we go somewhere I can get a drink?" Larry the Lush. That's what everyone calls him. He's an interesting guy, but oh man, can he ever drink, and drink, and drink...

"Sure thing. There's that place, what's it called? Up the street. They have really good coffee, and you can get wine there."

Larry grins again. "Oh wine! Perfect! Now honey, tell me all about it."

Annie smirks and raises one hand for Larry to take. "Lead on, Mister Lush."

Larry curtsies, raises his hand to Annie's, and hand over hand, they parade along the sidewalk up Haight. "Now Miz Monroe, you tell Auntie Lush aaaall about it. And oo, start from the very top, with *feeling*!"

"There may not be a Heaven, but there is a San Francisco."
– **Ashleigh Brilliant**

White Light

1

"Hmm hmm hmm..."

Quiet white light filters through the crepe paper streamered room. Everything is white. The bead-boarded walls are clean and white. The wood planked floor is painted a pale, dry talcumed white. So very white, and cool, and clean. Carla is sitting on a white painted steamer trunk in a corner of the room. There is no other furniture in the small, high-ceilinged space.

Carla is white too. Her hair has been bleached nearly translucent, paler than she thought possible. She has clean-shaven temples, nice and silky. She likes the feel of her skull on each side of her head. So smooth and bump-free. Her skin is pearlescent. She wears a stiff white sleeveless t-shirt, starched rigid as a plank, a little ragged at the edges. Her arms hang akimbo from their sockets, like a scarecrow oddly put together. Her underwear, in all this white, is black. Black and lacy and wet. The room smells of her sex.

She is pungent. Her scent is strong. She hasn't bathed in days, but that doesn't matter to her, not at the moment. She hasn't gone out, and no one has come in. She's been in the apartment, all two tiny rooms of it, for a long time, alone. She's been shooting speed and decorating, painting everything white, and arranging her things in precise little rows and angles. Well, and the other...

Before she started this binge, she'd gone out and bought all the supplies she thought she would need: five gallons of varying shades of white paint, rollers and brushes, a beautiful white speckled drop cloth that she thinks she'll leave on the floor where it lies rumpled against one wall, and a quarter ounce bag of lovely speed.

She'd received her monthly stipend from the lawyers, and decided to spend it on herself instead of throwing it around like she normally does. She stuffed all her billowy 1950's prom dresses into the one small boxy closet just to the right of her front door, gave away all her furniture except for the trunk, and bleached and cut her hair. Ready at last, she called Annie and arranged to meet up with her at Café Greco down the street.

At a small marble-topped table, she palmed the large bag of speed over demi-tasses of espresso, and murmuring distracted gratitude over Annie's flirtatious exclamations of romance, paid for the coffee and meth, and left.

Now she's been making her way through her queenly purchase, getting so much done, yet doesn't feel like she's accomplished what she set out to do. She's not exactly sure how to get there, but she'll keep trying until she works it out. Daddy didn't raise a loser. Meanwhile, the apartment looks *perfect*, so clean and pure... And the time alone has been...well, interesting.

After she'd finished painting, powdering and draping streamers around the apartment, she'd come across her vibrator in one of the kitchen drawers, and decided to get some use out of it. She'd owned the damned thing for over a year and never turned it on. Now it's going both ways, the turning on, that is.

So she's been staying inside, shooting speed, and jacking off. She fantasizes as she goes to work on herself. Sometimes she can use the same fantasy four or five times in a row before needing something new and unknown. She twists the vibrator on and regards the white room through half-closed eyes. Scenes play in her mind against the white screen of the walls. Sometimes she even sees things-people, and places for real, the speed is that good.

When the batteries run out, she throws them away. She

inserts new, fresh batteries she has stored in her freezer into the vibrator shaft, and hums. She smiles to herself, "How many is that?" She's trying to set a record for the most number of consecutive orgasms in one sitting. She's not sure what the number is, but she's sure she's beating it. At least she's beating something, she thinks to herself.

"Hmm hmm hmm..."

She feels a new fantasy coming on. In this fantasy, she is a dog, a big, black dog. A Doberman, she thinks. And she is in heat, sure, why not?! All these boy dogs come sniffing around for miles. Her heat is driving them crazy. Her scent makes them howl and scratch at the dirt.

She slips down off the steamer trunk, and lands on the floor with a small thunk. She scratches her back on the trunk's main brass latch, but she can't stop now. She's just starting up. The boy dogs must fight one another to see who will have the honor of fucking her. She watches them, wary, half interested. The heat bears down heavily on her eyes and skin. It burns at her legs and raises her fur into a ridge along her spine. She flips over and raises her rump high into the air, begging that other big black Doberman to come and take her. She sees him, sees the ring of dogs keeping their distance beneath the wide, blue sky.

She begins to whine, a small harmonic whimper that bounces off the empty walls. Her legs start to shake, and she pushes them, heels flat, against the trunk. The vibrator is going full throttle now, vibrating hard and loud, cutting out the sounds of the street below. Carla balances herself on one arm and both knees, her other arm tucked tightly against the length of her body, working the vibrator firmly, slickly, back and forth.

The other big black dog turns out to be another bitch. It is a bigger, blacker, Doberman female. She doesn't have to fight the other dogs to get here. She just prances right on past them as they circle one another, and sashays elegantly to where Carla is about to orgasm. Ooohhh... here it comes...

The boy dogs don't notice the other Doberman. She doesn't smell of heat and sex, or hormones ready to rumble. She's still interested though. And Carla gladly welcomes her. She shoves her rump into the other Doberman's nose. It is wet and cold, oh sweet God. The other Doberman begins to shake too. She licks at Carla's rump with her warm, rough tongue. The vibrator whines on and on.

Carla feels that sweet, familiar pain start to come over her. This is a pain she loves. It rolls inside her, slowly, shifting direction, moving ever upwards and spreading throughout her groin. Suddenly it twists without warning and jumps up to snatch at her clit. She trembles and falls forward onto her shoulders, turning her face to one side, and panting short, ragged, deep breaths. She rolls over onto her back. The Doberman has disappeared. The universe has narrowed down to Carla and her vibrator alone.

Carla slows the vibrator down, riding the waves of orgasm as they overtake her. She moans and bucks at the instrument in her hand. Moving it slowly, deliciously, over the mouth of her vagina and her hard, raised clit, she writhes and squeezes her eyes shut tight. The pain has blown out her insides, empty and clean, her own personal A-bomb... She is truly on fire now, feels it blasting through her. Reverently, she orgasms, allowing its way with her, spreading from her clit to her small, pale, flat buttocks, her pert, pebble-like nipples, her toes, curled on point, the very hairs on the back of her neck raised up.

She twists the vibrator off and feels the small of her back relax into the hard, warm wood floor. She lays there, in a puddle of her own sweat and juice, consumed, steaming. A dull, persistent hammering slams at her sex, must be her heartbeat, she thinks. She holds the vibrator up to view its shiny plastic shell. It is slick, beaded with her orgasm. She reaches behind her and places the vibrator on its side, at the lip of the trunk above her.

The apartment is quiet now. Street sounds filter in through the open window, its sheer paneled curtains billowing slightly in the afternoon breeze. Carla turns her head towards the window and smiles to herself. There, wound loosely around the iron balcony railing, is the heavy chain and lock Gabe gave her last time he was here. He'd been wearing it, the lock nestled against the few straggling brown hairs on his chest, and after they kissed, he unlocked and removed it and wound it around the middle rail. He'd snapped the lock shut, gave her a sly sideways grin, then leaned back against the window frame and lit a Marlboro filter-less cig.

They hadn't kissed again after that, but then again, Carla is avoiding him. Afraid that he might think there's more to their fucking around than she wants, she stayed away from The Shits' next two shows and started this little adventure she is currently enjoying. Gabe has stopped by her place a few times, yelling up to her window from the street below. Carla ducked down and retreated to the tiny, narrow kitchen at the back of her place, waiting until he left each time.

One of these days, she'll have to see him. She can't hide here forever, and she has to see her friends, or go to a show sometime. Even if it's just to buy more speed. Fuck, why, Gabe? Carla shakes her head, no. She likes Gabe a lot, just not like she thinks he wants. She sighs out loud, a whisper more than anything. She doesn't like feeling out of control, so she keeps herself nice and distant. She likes to fuck. When there's flirting and kissing and all the good stuff, she feels right. She can walk away at any time. But she can tell that with Gabe... if she let him in, he could fall hard and get hurt so easily. And she can't have that.

Carla remembers when all this started. She rolls over and off her pooled juices. Leaning back against the trunk, she thinks about that day. She'd been walking from the corner store to Shelly's place. Shelly is another dealer in town. She dabbles in heroin as well as her regular stock of speed, but mostly she's known for her fairly decent supply of 'Up', as Carla likes to call it. Annie'd been occupied, or out of town. Carla doesn't remember which. Either way, she'd driven her shiny candy apple red Corvette over to Shelly's, realizing, as she looked for parking, what a mistake that was. Shelly lived across the street from the projects in a pretty dangerous neighborhood. Waving that car around that area was a bad idea. So she'd parked up on the other side of Divisadero, stopped in at the corner store for some licorice, and headed on foot towards Shelly's.

2

Carla doesn't remember where they came from, only that suddenly she was flanked on both sides by two project kids in their late teens. They were both black, that coffee color with a dab of cream, in shorn-to-the-head haircuts with bits of flyaway curls, and sore looking acne on both their chins. They each wore dark, new jeans and shiny dark blue nylon windbreakers, though the sun was out and shining hard for The City. She remembers thinking that. One of them, the kid with a wide, flat nose, and oddly thin lips, asked if she was going to visit her friend in the yellow house. Carla looked up and noticed for the first time. Shelly's place was painted yellow: a soft, buttery, flaking, peeling yellow. All Carla had noticed before was the grey porch and heavy iron bars covering all the windows. She threw her thin shoulders back.

"That's none of your business."

"Huh! Woo! Yeah, actually, it *is*," the same kid snapped back.

Carla reached one hand into her skirt waistband as though to scratch herself and wrapped her fingers around the hilt of the navy issue knife she kept strapped there.

"Oh *really*?" The other teen with his tilted lovely eyes and heart-shaped lips leaned his body around to partly block her way. "You wanna play with knives? How about we play with *this* too, and see how that goes?" He pulled his hand slightly out of his windbreaker pocket, revealing a dull black snub-nosed gun. Carla didn't know anything about guns, but she knew enough to know what one looks like.

"Why don't you hand your little butter knife over, and we'll just keep walking like friends?" The first teen held out his hand, glancing from his friend back to her, his eyes serious and dark. Carla hesitated. The first teen put one hand on her back, threatening now. "Hand it over."

Carla unsnapped the knife from its sheath and flipping it around so the blade rested in her palm facing her, offered the handle to him. He laughed. "Good girl!" Leaving his left hand on her back, he accepted the knife and pocketed it somewhere. They escorted her up to Shelly's house and paused at the foot of the four wide gray cement stairs. Carla shifted the small paper bag holding her licorice nervously from one hand to the next.

"Ok, so go knock on the door and get them to let you in. You say one word about us being here, we kill you. Got it?"

Carla nodded. She wished she hadn't pulled her knife out.

It was her favorite. And now it's gone. She walked up the stairs. The teens each moved to one side of the doorway, keeping flat against the front of the house and away from the peephole mounted in Shelly's door. Carla knocked.

She heard footsteps in the hallway behind the door, and heard a male voice call out. "Yeah! Just a sec!" A colored shadow fell across the peephole, as Carla stood there, trying to give a look of warning without being detected by the teens. She heard Gabe, Shelly's brother, call out, "Hey! Carla! Shelly's not here, but you can come in and wait if you want." He began to monkey with the locks.

Carla shook her head no, trying to remain imperceptible to the two teens. "No, that's ok. I can come back." She worked her eyes into a look that she hoped might seem foreboding and friendly at once. The teen with the gun, Pretty Lips, noticed. He motioned with the gun in his pocket and narrowed his eyes in warning. Carla spoke again, at the same time as Gabe.

"Well, ok... I can wait..."

"No really, it's cool. I'm just waiting too."

They both laughed, Carla nervously. Gabe unlocked the heavy bolt, slid the chain lock free, and opened the door.

Carla stood still, unsure what to do. The teens rushed at the door, knocking Carla into Gabe, and Gabe against the hallway wall. "Back off!" Wide Nose yelled. "Stay cool!" Pretty Lips said, to Gabe or Carla, or maybe to his friend, and pulled the door shut behind them. He pushed Carla down the hall, Wide Nose backing him up. Pretty Lips now had the gun pulled out of his pocket and was waving it wildly at the wall, the floor, Carla, the wall again.

"Where's the stuff, man?"

He shoved Carla towards the first door to the right of the long hallway. She tried to glance back at Gabe, standing uncertainly near the front door. "Oh no ya don't!" Pretty Lips spun around and pointed it at Gabe. "Get AWAY from the door, man." Wide Nose, closest to Carla, reached around her and opened the hall door, pushing her through the doorway and into the room behind it. Two punks Carla knew from shows, not that well, but by sight, sat on the bed, eyes suddenly wide in amazement and fear. They were all obviously waiting for Shelly to get back from her drug run, or wherever she was. Carla felt that palpable sense of urgent, nervous impatience found in drug houses everywhere. At least, all the drug houses she'd been to. It was quickly replaced by a rapidly blossoming scent of surprise and fear.

Wide Nose kicked the door shut. They heard hard

scuffling and low grunts in the hallway. Then SLAM! The walls and door shook when someone hit something, a wall it sounded like, out there. She heard Gabe saying something unintelligible, and the sound of a toy gun, going Pop! Pop! One of the punks, hands dangling over both knees in faded black chinos and a dark grey short-sleeved mechanic's work shirt, narrowed his eyes and groaned. "Oh man... you're fucking *kidding* me. You guys use a... *toy* gun?"

Wide Nose looked wildly around the room, his eyes lighting on a jumble of pocketbooks and makeup kit bags on the settee to the right of the doorway. He grabbed them all and swung the door open, shoving Carla out of the way once again, onto the bed. Clutching the bags to his chest, he ran down the hall and yelled at his friend to follow. They threw the front door open and were gone in the slap of tennis shoes down the steps and onto the street.

Suddenly it was so quiet. Carla undraped herself from where she was tossed on the cold brass rail of the bed's footboard and peeked out the door, slammed open and partway shut again on its hinges. Gabe lay crumpled across the hall floor, groaning, holding his head in one hand. Carla leapt into the hallway.

"Oh my god, you guys! He's been shot! I think..."

The two punks jumped up and ran into the hallway behind her. Carla knelt by Gabe, and was joined by the quiet punk- a large gal, with a limp, Hitler-ish Mohawk that lay flat against her forehead, dressed in an oversized Sex Pistols t-shirt and camouflage cut-offs. The other punk, his hair spiked in short, fat blades all over his head, stood over them. Gabe groaned again.

"That's impossible. That was a toy, wasn't it?" The large punk asked. She looked intently at Carla.

Carla shrugged, "Hmm." She didn't know guns. She *thought* it sounded like a toy. She searched Gabe's face for signs of blood, a wound, anything out of place. She lifted his hand from his face and held it, suspended, ten inches over his head. She had no idea what to do. There was no blood anywhere. And oh man, she'd only wanted to buy some speed. Simple. None of this crazy drama, thank you. And where was Shelly with all this going on?

"Hey... there's a bullet hole here."

Carla and the large punk looked up. The spike-haired guy, what *was* his name, Carla asked herself, pointed to a small hole in the antique parlor-papered wall above their heads. She released Gabe's hand and stood up.

"Really? That was *real*?"

The large gal stood too, everyone standing over Gabe and squinting at the wall. The bullet hole was tiny, the size of a pencil eraser. Carla felt the hairs on the back of her neck stand up. The low level of fear in the hallway and its' accompanying rush suddenly intensified. Carla heard a dark buzz in her ears, when her knees buckled from underneath her and she tumbled against the wall. She slid down onto the floor next to Gabe and bit her lower lip. All she'd wanted was to cop. Both punks stared at her, waiting to see what might happen next. She looked up.

"Can either of you drive a stick?"

The two punks looked at one another and back down at Carla. The large gal spoke up. "I can. Why?"

Carla edged away from Gabe a few inches, realizing she was crowding him there on the floor. "I... I'm feeling too shaky to drive, but I thought one of you could take my car and take Gabe to the hospital. It's just down the street. The car, AND the hospital." She looked down at her hands, which were trembling now.

The large punk nodded, "Sure, I can do that. I know where

the hospital is, up off Diviz, right? Where's your car? Where's your keys?"

The spike-haired punk stepped back. "I'll wait here for Shelly." The large gal smirked. "Right. Don't do any till we get back. That's *my* money, Derek." Derek turned away and stuffed both hands into the front pockets of his chinos. He turned around again and leaned against the opposite wall. "No prob."

Carla fumbled with her skirt pocket until she was able to retrieve her car keys, attached to her lucky plastic Pink Panther pawprint. Not so lucky today. She handed them up to the large punk, *Becky, that's* her name*!* "It's up on the other side of Divisadero, around the corner to the right, I think, on Broderick." She reached over to Gabe. "I'll stay here with Gabe while you get the car. When you're out front, honk, and we can load him up."

Becky swung the keys into the air and caught them. "What kind of car am I looking for?"

Carla looked up, glanced quickly at Derek, then smiled, "A red Corvette." She pulled her hand away from Gabe's shoulder and noticed the crumpled bag of licorice on the floor by the front door. Becky whistled, "Whew! How the hell did you get *that*?"

Carla cleared her throat. She turned over onto her knees and reached around Gabe's head placing one hand on each of his shoulders, trying to lift him up slightly, so he could lean against the wall in a sitting position. He helped her by pushing himself up from the floor and leaning back again.

"I have this inheritance. My great-grandpa is George Eastman. He's the guy who started Kodak, so I got a lot of money when I turned eighteen. Well, I get an allowance sort of. Anyway, it's a cool car, but you know, parking is a bitch."

Becky snorted, "Yeah, I guess. Damn, must be nice… ok, I'm outta here." She gave Carla a reassuring smile and ran out the door. Derek pushed himself away from the wall and sauntered into the back room off the hallway again, hands hidden deep in his pockets, shoulders tightly lifted, as though he were cold. Carla touched Gabe's forehead. It seemed hot, but that could have been her. *She* felt cold, come to think of it. Gabe raised one hand to his head, brushing Carla's hand away.

"Am I hot? I don't feel hot, but I *do* feel… fuck. Like my head's gonna explode."

Carla stood a little uneasily, her knees still weak. "Let me get you a wet washcloth or something." She glanced back over her shoulder to where Derek had retreated. "*He* won't be much help. Do you need anything else? Something to drink?"

Gabe chuckled, then wrapped his fingers around his forehead. "Owww... yeah, don't make me laugh. I was about to say, yeah, a shot of whiskey. But no, I'm ok. Thanks."

Carla moved down the hall to the single, disturbingly dirty bathroom, tiled in those cool little hexagon-shaped tiles she loved so much. Too bad they were so caked with hair, fuzz, spatters of toothpaste, soap and who knows what else. What, did Shelly have a monkey or something? Carla found a piece of towel, cut from something larger, sniffed it, and finding it not *too* rancid, moistened it and brought it back out to Gabe in the hall.

They waited there, side by side, for what seemed like a long time. Carla thinks back, it must have been only about five minutes. However long it took though, it was long enough for Carla and Gabe to somehow connect in a way she hadn't foreseen. She'd never thought of him that way before. He was just one of The Shits, big deal. Big punk rock star around town. Shelly's brother. Just another guy, really. But here he was, all sensitive and thanking her, sort of needy, and sort of sexy. Whatever it was, Carla found herself liking it. She felt a little zing in the back of her throat, almost like she felt when she shot speed. Only this was unexpected. She knew what she was getting into when she gave herself a shot.

The horn honked outside, and Carla stood again, holding onto Gabe's arm, feeling heat pass between them as she helped him to his feet. He leaned against her, one arm draped over her shoulder, as she walked him out the door and down the shady cement steps to the bright cherry red car, double-parked out front. She held onto the top of his head as he lowered himself into the nearly reclined passenger seat, a natural move, like they do on TV. She closed the door behind him, and realized she was a bit turned on, as Becky drove off slowly, riding the clutch a little too long.

3

Carla walked back inside just as Shelly came running up the sidewalk. "What the FUCK?! What the hell is going ON here?!" She spit as she raved, tiny bits of saliva spewing from her tongue and lips. She demanded to know what had happened. Her eyes were comically enormous, the irises spinning slightly, as though she'd just come off a mad merry-go-round. Carla filled her in on what had happened and let her know where Becky and Gabe had gone off to. That Gabe seemed like he was fine- he hadn't been shot - but that they'd taken him to the hospital for what was most likely a concussion. Also that Derek was still waiting in her room. Also, come to think of it, the two guys who'd broken in, they'd both seemed *really* nervous. More nervous than anyone else there. Rookies, Carla decided.

Shelly grabbed onto Carla's arm as they walked into her place. She dug her fingers into Carla's flesh so that Carla had to squeak a little, let her know it hurt. They walked down the hall to the kitchen at the back of the apartment, sunny and yolkish, despite it being hidden so far behind so much of the building. Shelly pulled out her electric blue pager and showed Carla- someone had paged her right as the theft was happening. They'd entered 666, then 911, then 666 again. And the return number, where the page had originated, was Shelly's apartment, her home number.

Carla assured her that no one had called. They both looked at one another in fear, frozen, waiting for someone to tell them what had happened there, and what to do next.

Carla remembered, "One of the guys got your stuff, I think." She walked back down the hallway to Shelly's room. Shelly followed her, overtook Carla at the doorway, and rushed inside. "I don't have any stash here. I was out, copping..." Carla pointed to the now-empty settee to the right of the door. Shelly paused as she took in what Carla was pointing at, then doubled over and started laughing out loud.

"Oh ho ho!! That?!" She looked up over her shoulder at Carla. "That was a bunch of makeup and stuff I had piled up there! They fucking broke in and stole a bunch of *makeup*?!"

She swung her shoulder-length thin black hair out of her eyes and stood up straight again. "Oh *man*!" Shelly glanced over at Derek, sitting slumped over both knees at the edge of Shelly's bed. "No, they didn't get a thing, besides some old crappy mascara and Avon samples my mom gave me." She paused, placed her hands on her waist then turned to Carla. "S'weird that Gabe was here. He never comes to visit."

Carla agreed. They left Derek and returned to the kitchen

where Shelly began to weigh out her wares. Shelly dumped a healthy taste onto a small square of mirror she pulled from one of the kitchen cabinets and urged Carla to partake a little, in thanks for offering up her car. Carla blushed, but didn't say no. Contrary to Reagan's little ditty, she'd learned, never say no to drugs.

Gabe and Becky returned about an hour later with nothing surprising to share. Gabe had been pistol-whipped, so he had a slight concussion and should rest. Becky had parked the car on the corner in the yellow zone, and *loved* driving it. Anytime Carla needed a chauffeur...

Gabe and Carla locked eyes. Even as high as she was, she felt it again, that tingle in her throat. Shelly offered the mirror around, and Carla took a second taste. Gabe held the mirror for her, and she for Gabe. That was a little sappy, but what the hell, flirting is a hit all on its own... No one else seemed to notice. Carla opened the box of licorice and passed that around. Gabe looked like a candy cowboy from the wild west with the limp red whip dangling out of his mouth. Quite kissable, actually...

Becky and Derek retired to the dingy bathroom to shoot their free taste. Carla decided she'd stayed long enough. Besides, she didn't need her car getting towed, again. So she hugged Shelly goodbye, rapped on the bathroom door and called out 'see ya' to the two, busy at their task, inside. She slipped the half-empty box of licorice into its' rumpled bag, touched the small bag of speed in her skirt pocket, and walked expectantly towards the front door. Gabe followed, fingers tapping on the wall behind her.

"So, uh... thanks. For the ride and all." He leaned on the wall, shadowing her, the knuckles of one hand pressed up against his lips. Carla smiled nervously. Her lips were dry and stuck to her upper teeth. She crinkled the bag of candy in her hands and bounced her shoulder blades lightly against the wall, looking up into Gabe's eyes. *Do it, already...*

"Sure," she shrugged. She looked down for an instant, then back up at Gabe, his mouth, the curve of his lips, his eyes... Gabe grinned.

"So, ok. Why don't you and me get together so I can thank you properly? Buy you a drink, or take you to Double Rainbow for some ice cream, you name it." A flicker of doubt flashed across his eyes. Carla smiled, more broadly, her lips and teeth unsticking. *Now that's more like it.*

"Sounds good. You know where I live?"

"No. Where's that?"

Carla pursed her lips in mock prudishness. "Well... I *suppose* it's ok to let you come over. I live across the street from the Savoy on Grant. Upstairs apartment above the little crappy Chinese grocery there? There's that cool postcard store across the street too, next to the Savoy. You know it? They have weird cards, like, collectibles from the 40's and 50's, and weird science fiction stuff. Trippy place. Um, anyway, my buzzer doesn't work, so you have to yell. I leave my window open so I can hear you, just in case I'm in the back or something."

Gabe grinned harder. "Perfect." He touched his free hand to his forehead, still leaning on the one arm, closing Carla into a shadowy corner. "Once this feels better, I'm there. That's a warning."

Carla smiled and thought ahead to what they'd do. Gabe pushed himself off the wall and stepped back to hold the door open for her. She stepped out into the bright day. "See you Gabe. I hope you feel better soon." She laughed, slightly sinister, definitely aroused. He nodded, "Yup. See you, Carla." He winked and shot both hands at her in a double fire 'bang bang' of fingers on the triggers of two invisible handguns. Carla shook her head no no no... Oh, Gabe... He winced as he realized what he'd just alluded to, and raising his eyebrows and shoulders up in a 'forgive me' gesture, shut the door behind him.

Carla sighs and rolls over again on the floor. She places two fingers in her mouth, tasting herself, her heart beating cooler now, gentler, more of a soft wave than the crashing she'd felt only moments before. She sucks her fingers dry and rolls onto her back, stretching her arms above her head. The whole room whispers with the soft afternoon wind. Footsteps thud up the stairs and back down again. Her landlord's kids must be playing in the stairwell. Someone calls out to someone else from the street below. She begins to notice the sounds of traffic and humanity outside her apartment window. Buses growl, horns meep and wonk, the city comes to life for her, the first time in how many days...

Carla looks around her place, so white, so cool, so clean. Streamers of crepe paper flutter and spin, hanging from the ceiling and fan. The sun casts pale shadows from the sheer curtains onto the opposite wall. Her scent fills the room. She thinks, ok, maybe it's time to shower. That was number one hundred and ninety-two. That *has* to be a record! She remembers reading somewhere someone having one hundred and twenty five in a row in one hour. There's no way she could do *that*, but one hundred ninety two, that'll do.

Carla firmly decides, yeah, she's ready to call it good. Maybe she'll get out and take some pictures. Maybe she'll go to some construction site and do some exploring. She thinks about it for a while, then sits and pushes herself up onto her feet. She looks at the vibrator lying there on the trunk and picks it up. This baby needs a shower too.

She walks into the next room, separated from the smaller front room by a sliding pocket door. Leaving the door open, she notices dust bunnies rolling around in the afternoon breeze, and doubles over, chasing after them. She brushes dust and white hair off the vibrator and tosses it into the trashcan, just inside her tiny bathroom's doorway. She places the vibrator upright on its' end, on the scalloped bathroom sink, and turns back to the main room.

Carla marches over to the wall opposite the bathroom, to her favorite thing about this apartment: the built-in wood cabinets, with their leaded glass fronts and tracked rolling Murphy bed. Rifling through one of the drawers to one side of the bed, now put away and pushed into its hidden wall socket, Carla selects a new, fresh pair of black panties. She opens another drawer and pulls out a pair of short, short denim cut-offs. She's going Daisy Duke today. Tucking the clean clothes beneath one thin arm, she sniffs her fingers again. She is strong, she thinks, and that is good.

She lays the fresh, clean clothes on the floor outside the bathroom, sheds the stiff, soaked t-shirt and panties into another pile, and steps into her clean, glowingly bright bathroom. Carla showers, a long, steamy hot scrub that washes away all her scent and most of the speed's residue oozing through the pores of her arms, chest and face. Really, it's all over her, but that's where she notices it most. At least she doesn't pick that often, like some of her friends out there walking around with bloody little scabs picked in clumps around the backs of their arms, or across the bridges of their noses. Carla is careful to occupy her hands otherwise. Hence the apartment project, and the aim for that orgasm record. Most often, she stalks the streets, taking pictures of shadows, people, building angles and whatever else catches her eye.

She steps gingerly from the shower, carefully placing each foot firmly on the ground before taking the next step. She feels like a fresh young foal, taking its' first steps in the world. All that speed, I guess, will make you feel *something*, she thinks. Speaking of which... she's starting to come down, to feel a shadowy caul ease over her mind and vision. Time for another shot! She hums happily to herself.

Carla dresses, heading back to the rumble bed to choose a new shirt. She pulls one of her favorites out of the pile of shirts roughly folded in another drawer. No t-shirt for picture taking, no sir! She dons the worn-thin tuxedo shirt with the tear across the back exposing her bat tattoo, and the panties and shorts. She turns around and around in front of the full-length mirror that leans against the wall next to the bathroom. She can barely see the shorts, they're that short, and with the tuxedo shirt hanging down just to there- she eyes the tops of her legs- it looks like she's not wearing pants at all. She likes it.

Carla glances around the room, at the overflowing ashtray on the floor by the base of the bed, at the double and triple-rowed stacks of books in the leaded shelves above. Carla likes books, especially odd ones that you just don't see anywhere. She has a complete collection of Blue Boy books, biographies on her personal heroes like Diane Arbus and Jane Bowles, an anatomy coloring book, and books about Buddhism, Hinduism, Taoism, and other religions. Carla has been searching for answers for years but hasn't found them yet in a book. Still, she keeps looking.

Her camera, a nice new Nikon F1, is tucked in its case to one side of the bottom-most leaded glass fronted shelf. Satisfied with her next project, Carla does a little jig, and dance-walks into the kitchen, reaching her hands up to touch the fluttering, spinning crepe paper streamers on her way there. There is something superstitious about the way she touches the streamers. She needs to allow her fingers to linger on each piece of crepe for two seconds, counting 'one, two' out loud, then moving onto the next. She dances along to the count, and eventually makes it to the kitchen door. Carla has an eerie feeling that if she doesn't handle each piece of crepe like that, then some evil spirit will come into her home and occupy it. She knows if anyone knew about these thoughts, they would make fun of her. But still, she's done this sort of thing for years without anyone knowing, keeping the evil spirits at bay by genuflecting, counting for them, turning this way and that as they expect of her, and nothing bad has happened yet. She's kept the spirits happy so far.

4

Now it's time for another shot. Spirits happy? Check. All scrubbed and clean? Check. Apartment looking perfectly the way she'd imagined it? Check. Record level of orgasms? Check! Let me at this day, she thinks. I'm ready to hit the street. Her hands shake slightly in anticipation. She walks over to her set-up, arranged just-so on the counter by the sink. Carla opens the colorful tin box, its lid snapping open with a tiny 'tock'. She removes the carefully folded and refolded packet of speed, now reduced to over half what she'd bought. Was that last week? The other day? What day is it anyway? What month?

She untapes the cellophane and the packet unfurls into her hand. A quick, bitter scent whisks into the air, filling her nostrils with the promise it always offers. She rolls the edge of the baggie between her fingertips, opening its' little mouth wide. Tiny crystals slide over one another like sand inside the bag. This stuff is really good. Carla smiles and taps at the bag with her free hand. She hates this. She loves it too. She can't think of anything else she'd rather do. Sorry daddy.

Carla touches the spoon laid out so neatly along the row of specific instruments lined up there on the counter. She carefully tips the baggie over the spoon and pours out a decent amount into its' shiny bowl. She taps straggling grains of speed back down into the bottom of the baggie, and folds it back up, pressing the tape down with a firm thumb. Her heart is racing fast now, faster than her hands can move. She blinks to clear her vision and focuses her eyes on the spoon. Even with the bright daylight spilling into the kitchen from the window above the sink, it seems darker, almost dim, compared to the two front rooms. Carla reaches over and flips the light on, yet still her vision wavers, swimming and hazy.

She pops the orange plastic top off of her precious needle, the last from the box she'd scored off the street a month or so ago. Carla feels the fillings in her mouth creak and grind in anticipation. She fills a low-rimmed white ceramic bowl with water from the tap. Lowering the needle into the shallow water at a slant, she pulls back on the light gauge plunger, still brightly lettered and numbered. The needle is still sharp too, good enough for now.

The plunger resists a little as she pulls back on it, which is not good. With the needle full, Carla turns to the sink and pushes down on the plunger. She refills the needle and empties it again. The plunger loosens up a little; there must have been some residue from her last shot. Amateur... the last plunger-full shoots into the sink in a steady piss of silvery light. Carla's face has settled into a grim mask of concentration. If anything, she is paler than usual.

She lowers the needle into the dish again and fills it to the ten CC mark. She points the tip of the needle into the spoon at an angle and lets the water drip forcefully, slowly, onto the good stuff there. The crystals melt quickly, merging into one luscious pool of good times. Oh how clean this batch is. Her face softens. Carla's body warms to the melting crystals. She easily performs the next well-practiced steps leading her towards her awaited shot, feeling it, like the sun warming her veins. She moves quickly, yet steadily. Not a single motion is wasted. That's the best part about shooting up, Carla would say if asked. Everything has its' place and moment. The ritual must be exact.

Carla swirls the speed around with precise motions in the spoon. Her world has shrunk down to this, and just this. She tears a bit of cotton from a swab in the tin box. She rolls it tightly between her thumb and forefinger and drops it into the spoon. It quickly wets and engorges, filling her mouth with a sweet, metallic taste.

Everything has become one. Carla, her projects, Gabe and sex and whoever else she hones in on... Carla presses the needle tip against the cotton, and slowly pulls back on the plunger. She watches the needle fill, and suddenly wishes she'd invited Sophie or Kelly-Belly over to share and go on an adventure with her. Too late now, there's other times, she figures. Her eyes grow large and wet with anticipation. Her lips press firmly, dryly closed.

The needle has sucked up every last drop from the cotton. Carla notes with satisfaction the tiny crust of white around the basin of the spoon, showing high water levels from this shot. She'll lick that after she's done. She hears Patty Smith's 'Horses' run through her mind and says 'Oh yeah... ' out loud. She holds the needle up, taps it, and feels a shiver run down her spine.

Carla lays the needle down, reluctantly releasing it from her fingers for a moment, on the cool counter tile. She picks up the leather thong that lies coiled carefully nearby. Uncoiling it, she slides its' loop up and over her right arm, the one that has the least scarring, maybe the most available vein. She hopes. Carla quickly tightens the noose and places the fringed end between her teeth. The taste of leather is good and solid. It's keeping her from fainting right about now. She flexes the fingers on the hand of the arm that is bound. Pumping her fist a few times, she raises a vein, oh so slightly. That vein is about to go, she can tell. Carla slaps at it, and it rises angrily in response. Foolish vein, don't you know what's coming next?

Carla tugs the leather fringe back more tightly by turning her neck slightly away from her arm. She picks up the needle with her free hand and cradles it perfectly with her long, thin white fingers, laying the tip of the needle at the top of the vein. She can feel her heart beating at the edge of the leather thong, straining weakly to pump around it. Carla pauses, one breath, then slides the needle slowly and cleanly, right into the heart of that poor, angry vein.

'Mark!' She imagines someone yelling out. 'Horses! Horses! Horses!' She hears Patti Smith singing. She wishes she had thought to put that record on, it would be so perfect to hear that sound swelling around her right now. The needle pinches a little, so it is dulling after all. Carla pulls back on the plunger, and the gorgeous cloud of pale red stuff billows into the needle's tiny shaft. She grimaces a little, feeling her heart jump. She pulls back a tad farther on the plunger then turns her fingers deftly and pushes it in. She releases the leather from between her teeth and spits the fringe out. The noose loosens around her upper arm, oh here comes the flow. She coughs, a small exhalation of air forced out from deep inside the back of her heart and lungs.

Oh my. Oh yes. This is what we came for. This is what it always is: the rush slams into Carla's brain, a speeding car, a bullet ricocheting off her skull, a runaway train. She closes her eyes and grasps the rounded lip of the kitchen counter with one hand, swaying in her new chemical tide. It carries her away. It lifts her up. It opens her heart and mind and turns her on. She begins to sweat, tiny trickles running down her ribs beneath both arms. The white light rushes through her entire body, spreading her toes apart. She can feel the speed opening her hips, straightening her back, making her stretch and stand up taller.

Automatically, Carla rinses her needle and restacks her kit in a neat row, all precise angles and everything pointing in one direction, up, away from her, towards the kitchen wall. Nothing touches. Everything has its' own space and place. Carla's feet begin to sweat on the cold, clean kitchen floor. She looks down, noting happily the absence of crumbs, dirt, dust bunnies, in here. Her kitchen is her lab. She never cooks except for cinnamon toast. She sees the cool, narrow tiled room as her workspace. She sets up and knocks down projects in here, kicking them off with shots of speed, given with Kodak precision every time.

Often, she'll start a binge off by shooting up then cleaning the kitchen thoroughly. She is thorough and obsessed. She scrubs the walls, light fixtures, tops of cabinets, backs of drawers. She can't relax into whatever her planned project is until the lab is neatly honed to a sparkling, steaming perfect shine, reeking of ammonia and lemon scented cleaning supplies. Once spotless, the lab releases Carla, and she can skip off to a day with her camera, or a book of crosswords, or night on the town.

She looks around, her fingertips resting lightly on the hard, gleaming counter tiles. The kitchen is already clean. She's been shooting and masturbating for so many days, she's scrubbed this room two or three times, she can't recall how many. So, time to shove off. She hesitates, unused to following her ritual by leaving. She picks up one of the two sponges lying against the back rim of the sink and runs it lightly over the outer edge of the sink area, picking up any stray drops of water that might have scattered there from her needle. There are none, but just to be safe...

Satisfied that the room is truly clean, Carla replaces the sponge, turns off the light, and leaves everything as it is. Perfect, though something nags at her. She walks into her bedroom, and floats through, her mind already engaged with what is outside. At the pocket doors, she pauses, returns for her camera and a few rolls of film, and lightly trips her way back to the front room again.

Looking out the windows, she notices the quality of light outside. The day is just starting to fade. There is that grayish, faintly blue-tinged color reflecting off the buildings across the street. Carla likes that light. She'll adjust the f-stop and aperture and have some fun. White light inside, blue light out. This is going to be a good time, no matter where or when it starts.

5

Whenever she goes out, she takes her camera. Punks around town rarely see her without it. She used to bring it on drug buys, but after the one time she was at a friend's and some punk demanded she give him her camera, she started leaving it at home when scoring. Otherwise, it's with her all the time.

She usually takes photos at night, of unconscious or at least unaware, alcohol-addled bums in the park, of shadowy people walking beneath buzzing streetlights, of punks double-imaged at shows, throwing themselves around in a near-religious frenzy, of body parts, her friends' cheekbones, elbows and spines. Carla's photos are disturbing. They speed past one's eyes, a blur of image and color, subject and form. People often see different things in a photo, and have to revisit it, go back over the image to make sure what they thought they saw before they can agree on it.

Carla sees the world that way. Her vision is filled with that white light she loves so well, casting hard bright lines against the camera's eye, or more shadowy waves of color and sound, captured as blurred wisps of people in action, places on the move. What she shoots, she sees, and her photos are good. She displays pieces in the various cafes around North Beach and she had a show at one foo-foo gallery downtown, but never again. She felt out of control there, unable to show her photos the way she envisions them being seen. Also, the attention was directed at her as George Eastman's great-granddaughter, and not on her pictures themselves, so nope.

People still ask her to show again, to sell her photos through this gallery, or that one. But Carla can't work under pressure like that and she can't explain why. She shoots speed, takes on projects like the one where she painted her entire apartment white, and takes photos when she feels the drive to do so.

Lately, she's been hanging Xeroxed copies of her photos on light poles around The City, in North Beach, in the Haight, on Polk. She shellacs them onto the cold metal poles, where they fade with weather and time, or staples them, fifty staples per photo, onto aging wood poles here and there. Her photos are considered iconic- capturing this unique time and place in the City. The funky little card shop across the street from her apartment even carries a series of postcards of them, badly copied, but there they are. They have no idea she is the artist, and she doesn't mind.

Often, as Carla walks down the street, she sees people staring at her work. She hangs back, admiring them admiring her work. Alone, safe, and un-judged. She likes her life that way.

Her last fuckbuddy, the one before she started this new flirtation with Gabe, couldn't understand why Carla was so distant, so pre-occupied with her camera. He begged her to spend more time with him. He demanded it after a while. He tried to beat it out of her, to break her camera in two, but none of it worked. Carla wouldn't budge. She couldn't. As long as she was in control, not under anyone's spell, she was fine. If she didn't *need* anyone, then she was safe from potential harm, just like daddy taught her.

But Buck wanted her to be there with him, all the time. Be there *for* him. All. The. Time. It drove Carla crazy. She couldn't work. She began hiding in her apartment, or at friends' homes. She would shoot speed and hide, turning out all the lights and cringing in a corner. Or in a closet at someone's apartment. Buck would come over. He would bang on the door and scream her name out from the street below. He would stomp around her friend's place, demanding to know if they'd seen her and where, threatening odd ideas about how he would prove to her how much he loved her, how much she really needed him. Carla stopped responding to his threats and pleas early on. She kept quiet, creeping around The City on the constant lookout for Buck behind her. She felt crazy and frightened.

She would clutch her camera in one hand and cower against the floor, the wall, the closet door, trying to make herself as small as possible. Speed helped. She felt shrunken, tiny, yet stronger on speed, and that helped a lot.

Buck the Fuck had always been volatile like that, all along. He'd wooed her at first, bringing her treats and odd finds he'd scavenged off the street. But she knew who he was from watching him at shows for some time before they got together, so she knew what she was in for. He liked to raise his voice to siren levels and scream at people. He liked to threaten his way around clubs and get what he wanted, even if he didn't really want whatever it was. He ripped people off, stole whatever he could, tried to get his way, one up on everyone around him.

Yet in the beginning, Buck had been so sweet to her. She liked the attention, and the books and things he found for her, so she allowed him in. She knew better, but she went along with him, despite her friends' warnings. She saw the burning building and walked in.

Carla knew that most of the gifts he brought her were either scavenged or stolen, including the drugs that he skimmed off the top of any deals he was in on. Carla didn't care. She kept her distance and accepted the presents. She would open the door to her place and there would be another box or envelope, gift-wrapped or topped with a bow. He was relentless, and for a while, she enjoyed it.

Once he became threatening and dangerous and she found herself recoiling so quickly, she realized she really didn't need anyone to bring her things. She could provide for herself, alone and capable of handling anything and anyone, just so long as she kept them at a distance. And with Buck, that meant a long distance.

After a while, he stopped harassing her. He found a new girl to trail and woo, and Carla liked that just fine. But he went ballistic one night. He raped this girl and left her to die behind Petrini's Market. Almost like he'd wanted to get caught, since he knew all the Clits stopped by there and ran through the piles of debris dropped off at the donation area nearly nightly. She didn't die though. She was found and taken to the hospital. She was ok now, but everyone whispered and pointed fingers. They should have seen this coming. They should have known.

After some quiet talks behind closed doors, Buck was run out of town. He'd ripped off one too many good folks, and this horrifying attack was the last straw. A loose-knit group of street-savvy punks got together and escorted him down to Palo Alto, where they left him at the side of the freeway with a torn, faded army pack filled with the few t-shirts and other bits he owned, and a warning not to come back through The City any time soon.

So now Carla is free to leave her apartment again. She visits her friends, goes to shows at the Mab up the street or over at the Tool & Die, and picks her way around The City, snapping photos whenever she pleases.

This morning, she'll trip through the streets, crossing and recrossing the road, sliding through the fog like a shadow herself, skipping along to the music playing in her head "How does it feel...". She'll hold her camera up to her eye, 'click', the shutter whirring open and shut as a rhythmic beat to whatever she's singing to herself. Each shot leads to the next. She follows her eye like she's following a trail, obviously set there for her alone to see.

"She trips out her front door for the first time in days. She stops, 'click', and moves on again. The City glimmers for her as a background to the visions she chases through the streets. She makes her way towards Polk, where Carla knows she'll find something new to interest her eye. Last time she was there, she crept along the walls of buildings and took pictures of men buying sex from other men. The way she took those pictures, no faces showed clearly, only runny shadows, fuzzy colors, trails of movement and blurred lines. Truly anonymous yet luminous, the same way she sees the world.

"San Francisco put on a show for me. I saw her across the bay, from the great road that bypasses Sausalito and enters the Golden Gate Bridge. The afternoon sun painted her white and gold---rising on her hills like a noble city in a happy dream. A city on hills has it over flat-land places. New York makes its own hills with craning buildings, but this gold and white acropolis rising wave on wave against the blue of the Pacific sky was a stunning thing, a painted thing like a picture of a medieval Italian city which can never have existed. I stopped in a parking place to look at her and the necklace bridge over the entrance from the sea that led to her. Over the green higher hills to the south, the evening fog rolled like herds of sheep coming to cote in the golden city. I've never seen her more lovely. When I was a child and we were going to the City, I couldn't sleep for several nights before, out of busting excitement. She leaves a mark."

– **John Steinbeck**

I Spy With My Little Eye

1

She doesn't see the man before she runs into him, bam! The side of her face smooshes softly up against cool leather and the cold hard teeth of a metal zipper.

"Whoa! Hey, hey! Slow down kiddo! What's the rush?"

Carla looks up from where she's been toying with her viewfinder. She knows this voice, rich and humorous, gilded with an edge of honey and smoke. She adores this man. Carla stops and smiles, and giggles apologetically.

"Aw Red. Sorry! You know what I get when I'm like this. Didn't mean to run into you. You ok?"

Red laughs in reply, a low rumble that starts deep in his belly and flies wide out of his throat. Carla can almost see the shape of it. She looks up and tilts her head to one side. Red's eyes glint with his smile.

"Nah, I'm fine, little sister. How you doing?"

Carla shrugs. "You know… high, low, high again. I'm good. I'm heading to Polk, to, you know, take some shots. Where are you going?" She holds her camera up to confirm that she is indeed, taking photos. Red smiles harder. His cheekbones are sharp, like arrowheads in his handsome redwood-dark face. His eyes slant glimmering and angled, startlingly blue above his Cherokee nose. His full, African lips open wide in an uncomplicated smile, amused by his jumpy and pale little friend. He nods.

"I'll join you. I was just out walking around. Nowhere to go, someone to be, you know how it is..."

They grin at each other; an adventure, of course. Carla feels deeply for Red. Not as someone she wants to conquer and fuck. She just really approves of him in every way. They've known one another a long time, always seeking each other out at shows. Whenever they spot each other across the room, they make their way through the crowd to take in the soft glow of their easy friendship. They've never asked too much from one another, just a cigarette every now and then, and a fun hang. It's never crossed Carla's mind to change that.

She likes the way he moves in the world, and he feels the same way about her. He's never asked her for a dime, though he, like everyone else, knows she has a lot of ducats. He feels protective of her and appreciates how she just is who she is. She doesn't put on any sort of attitude, so they respect each other and keep it clean.

Red places one massive arm against the wall. He cuts a sharp look down the street, and leans back against the moist brick, closing his eyes against the brightening daylight above them. Reaching into the inside pocket of his leather jacket, he pulls out a fresh new pack of Camel filters. He cracks the pack open and smacks it against the open palm of one hand, shaking a tightly packed cigarette out perfectly. He places the cigarette in his mouth, and grasping it with his lips, pulls it out of the pack. Dropping the Camels back into his jacket pocket, Red cups his hand expertly around the cigarette's end and lights it with the short red Bic lighter he had palmed in his other, free hand. He shakes his head.

"Shit. Sorry, want one?" Red holds the lit cigarette up in offering. Carla shakes her head, no. When she's this high, she doesn't like the taste of cigarettes. They feel grey and fuzzy in her mouth and throat, coating her tongue with smoke. They weigh her down with their heaviness, overriding her light chemical high. Red shrugs and bows slightly, extending one leg forward as he gazes, smiling around the cigarette in his mouth, into Carla's eyes.

"Alright then. Lead on, little sister."

Carla starts walking, and Red falls into step beside her. Carla asks, "So... you high? Cause, I'm gonna be spastic for a while. You know, don't want you getting bored."

Red smiles wryly. "Oh yeah, I'm cool. I was over at Annie's all night. She's got some new stuff in and Jesus it's good. Drew was there, and he and I spent the whole night talking about, God, I don't really know what. Gymnastics, logging, racecars... fuck, to tell you the truth, my head's in a blur. I couldn't give you a straight answer about anything right now. I mean, I'm high, but sorta wrecked. Don't know that I'll be much good company to you."

Carla giggles again, a painful, high cackle that scratches the back of her throat. She stops and leans against the rough brick wall. She coughs to clear her throat, and looks up at Red.

"Yeah, I know what you mean. I've been up for about 5 days now? I think anyway. What day is it?"

Red laughs again. "S'Thursday. You obviously are *not* working for the man!" He drags at his cigarette. "I'll hang until I start seeing things like in one of your pictures. Then I gotta go find a bed and crash."

Carla understands completely. There have been times when she has pushed her body and mind so hard that she doesn't know how she's still standing, let alone awake. But she keeps on until she drops. One time, she thought she was being followed by an alien disguised as a bush of some kind. Every time she peeked from the corner of her eye, she *knew* she saw it trailing her. She'd been far from home, all the way across town, and she'd felt so relieved to see the light on at her friend Steve's place. She'd knocked on the window to his ground floor apartment until he'd sheepishly pulled back the blinds. He'd been making it with his new boyfriend and Carla had interrupted. She couldn't deal with thinking about that at the time though. She'd been too freaked out by the alien bush.

Red has been homeless for about two months now. A few months back, his place burned down, and he hasn't settled anywhere new in that time. He's still trying to figure out what he wants to do- go home to Tahlequah down in Oklahoma, move someplace else in California, or find a new place in town. Los Angeles has been on his mind, but he's still undecided. He's a little unnerved by what happened, so he floats along from day to day, crashing at friends' places, and staying up all night, getting high.

A few months earlier, one of his roommates, Gerry, had been seeing a girl from a well-known hardcore witch coven from around town. She wore layers of black lace and heavily rimmed kohl around her eyes and lips and carried a book of spells with her everywhere she went. He'd become bored with her though- she didn't like to go to shows, she didn't like to party- so he'd abruptly stopped returning her calls and stopped calling her. He'd neglected to tell her about his change of heart, so she'd angrily stalked him, threatening spells and worse. He'd laughed and ignored her, and that was his big mistake.

One night, she came by the apartment where Red and his three roommates lived. She convinced another of Red's roommates to let her in, and crept up to the loft where Gerry roomed, bringing her book of spells along with her.

What happened next was pieced together by various accounts from those who were there, since the witch fled town after she was released from the hospital a few weeks later. Carla's not quite sure what to believe, but the fire was real, alright. That night, the witch cast a spell around the sleeping form of Gerry, surrounding his bed with candles, chalk drawings, and herbs. In the middle of her spell, his bed caught fire. And in her angry confusion, rather than put it out, she only managed to spread the flames further. Both she and Gerry ended up in the same burn ward at Saint Francis, which most likely made her feel connected to him once again.

Gerry survived the fire, but he was seriously injured. He's covered with second-degree burns over half of his body and needs skin grafts to replace most of his face. It will be some time before anyone sees him on the street again. Carla doesn't know him well enough to visit and isn't sure she could handle seeing such real damage on someone she knows at all, though maybe if she took pictures...

Everyone else in the building escaped with far fewer

injuries to tell their version of what happened that night. The flames quickly consumed the apartment, messy and filled with flyers, old furniture, and spray cans of paint that blew up as the fire engulfed them. The entire building was inhabited by low-income tenants, with cheap furniture and combustible housekeeping that fed the fire.

Red had been out and came home to find his street cut off by fire trucks, ambulances, and a police blockade. He lost everything in the fire- his clothes, books, music, bed, collection of punk rock show posters, everything gone. The American Red Cross had handed out checks to help replace burned clothing and personal items, and chits for a week's stay at a downtown hotel. Red hadn't used his yet, preferring to live off his friends for now. Someone, Carla can't remember who, some young street punk, had expressed such amazement that Red Cross would be so generous. Carla had to clarify that it wasn't the *band* Redd Kross, but the *institution*. Every time she sees Red now, she's reminded how grateful she is that he's ok.

Carla blurts out, "If you get too... ragged, you can go to my place. I just painted it this last week. You should see it!" She touches the tangled wave of white hair standing up around her head. "It's really... white. Kinda like..." She gestures to her hair, pulling on a strand for Red to see. "Do you like?"

Red blows smoke in a stream away from Carla. With his free hand, he reaches up and touches the crisp, blade-like shards of luminous white hair above her ear. It throws a shadow against her cheek.

"What, you use some kinda gel on this, sister? What the hell is this? Looks good, don't get me wrong, but dang! It's core!" He tries to bend one sharp point. It snaps slightly, and he stops. "Seriously, looks good. That is some serious shellac you got on there."

Carla reaches up to touch her hair where Red's hand had been. "Oh yeah. I used gelatin. You know, like for canning? It clumps a little, see..." She shows him the hard little pebble-like rocks of gelatin beaded up along her hairline. "But it works fucking great."

Red runs his hand along the short-cropped fuzz that covers his head. "I couldn't use that, ever. Wouldn't do a thing for me." He grins again and sucks on his cigarette. Carla smiles. Everyone calls Red by that name because of his naturally red hair. Shorn close to his head, pale and dusty-colored; in shadow, it seems darker. But here, outside in the clean light of day, it gives off a faint reddish halo. Carla has always approved of Red's hair- whether he allows it to grow slightly longer, like it is now, or when he shaves it all the way down. She realizes she doesn't know his real name, no one does, but that's ok. She loves him for being Red just the same.

She pushes off again. "So, uh... you seen Gabe around?"

Red hoots. "Oh yeah! I heard something about all that! The boy got pistol-whipped, right? And you were there!"

Carla double steps to catch up with Red's long, loping stride. "Yeah... it was scary. But you know what, I think the guys who did it were more afraid than we were."

She tells him all about what happened but doesn't mention the flirting thing between her and Gabe, nor the kiss. It didn't mean a thing in the end, so why mention it? The two friends fly high down the sidewalk, Carla's quick skipping steps keeping up with Red's athletic gait. People walking in the other direction clear a path around them. The two feel strong and invincible; they can feel the power flowing between them. They smile at their secret, how high they are, how illicit and perfectly shaped for The City, right here, right now. Carla snaps shots of Red's arm, raised to bring the cigarette to his mouth, of legs and feet, tangled in a walking city blur crossing the street, of a beautiful Vietnamese boy leaning against the outside of a bar, talking to a much older, balding white man.

On the corner of Polk and Clay, Red gestures and they turn

into the cool calm of a marble-tiled drug store. The sudden brisk air makes Carla shiver as they walk through the store to the wide glass-fronted fridge at the back. Carla grabs two blue Nehi's, daring Red to make fun of her, and pockets a pack of sugarless bubble gum. They head back up front to the single cashiered old-fashioned wood counter, and Carla pays for the two drinks. The bored clerk eyes Red with a hungry, seductive look. He wets his lips and flirts at the tall handsome dark man, but Red smiles nope, and carrying the two drinks, walks out.

Carla follows on his heels, shivering again from the cold. They walk into the moist heat of a perfect City morning and burst out laughing. "Man! I thought that guy was gonna try to take a bite out of you!"

Red sputters. "He *did* have some red lips, did you notice? Maybe he *does* bite some guys somewhere, just not me..."

Red pulls out his Swiss army knife, slightly pocked and rusty from years of use. He flicks out the bottle opener with one thumb and cracks open both Nehi's, handing one back to Carla. They hold up their bottles, 'clink' in a toast to being high together, and guzzle the sweet blue drink down.

Carla shifts the camera to one side slightly and looks down Polk Street. The morning street is different than the night street that she knows best. Small groups of men, young and old, gather outside closed bars and restaurants, making their way home to keep the party going. Carla feels conscious suddenly, that she has dragged Red here. He might feel uncomfortable, she wonders. She looks up at her friend, his lips stained blue.

"Hey. You wanna get off this street?"

Red looks back at her, a tiny furrow wedged between his eyes. "Why? Whatchya got in mind, lil sister?"

"I mean, I thought you might be uncomfortable. All these guys, you know... Are you ok with walking around on Polk? Don't you get freaked out by any of it? I mean, what if someone came on to you?"

Red chuckles. "Nah, I'm cool. One thing, they can look all they want. They just are *not* getting anything. Second, I'm hanging with you, so no one's gonna bother me. Trust me, that's the way it works. They'll look, and wish some, but no one's gonna touch." He finishes off the last dregs of his soda and tosses the empty bottle into the wire-rimmed can by a row of newspaper boxes along the street. Carla pushes off again, and Red falls into a slower step beside her.

Carla reaches into her pocket and pulls out the pack of

stolen gum. She unwraps the top and pulls out a piece, offering it to Red. He declines, too sweet, after all that sugary pop. She unwraps the piece and folds it in two between her teeth, chomping down, releasing a pink sweetness that coats her tongue perfectly, paired with the Nehi. As she drops her hand back to her side, the partly rolled sleeve of her tuxedo shirt falls back from her upper arm, covering the scars and bruises there. Red whistles and steps closer for a better look.

"Hang on a minute there, Carla. Let me see what you got going on here." He points at her arm, and she stops walking, and wrinkles her nose.

"No... you don't need to see this. I fucked up and kept chasing the veins in this arm. It's not pretty."

Red stands firm, with his feet planted wide apart. He crosses his arms in mock judgment. Carla sighs. "Okay, fine. Here." She holds her arm out for him to inspect, pulling back on the softly aged, starched white sleeve. The inside of her arm is a mess of mottled bruises and angry raised pustules. Red whistles again.

"Jesus lil' sister. You seriously abscessed there. Did you rub that in?" He gently touches one of the abscesses with his forefinger, rubbing it lightly back and forth. He can feel the liquid pebbled underneath the skin, hard, yet rolling slightly under his touch. A small line of tiny red dots runs up the inside of Carla's arm like footprints of little soldiers marching along the length of her veins. Her arm is so thin, so glaringly white, and so damaged. Red worries about her.

Carla winces and gently pulls her sleeve back down. "I know, I know. I had this stupid idea I could shoot all week and somehow not have to deal with any of this." She pauses and looks at her arm again. "Hell, I'll be asking Sheepvein for his doctor's name and number if I don't watch it." She grins, and Red chuckles too. Ok, so she knows she's hurting herself. At least that's something. Maybe she'll be more careful next time. Besides, there's a little bump of speed under the skin there, and as it releases, she'll continue to get high. That's always a plus.

"Sheepvein. Yeah, right. His doc should advertise. He'd make bank!"

Sheepvein is a part of the unofficial gang of punks who run the streets, live in squats and at the Vats, and can be found around town at shows and everywhere. He has a rare blood disease that prevents his blood from clotting normally, and sometime back- or so the rumor goes- one of his veins was replaced with a sheep's vein to restore the collapsed vein that he'd ruined by shooting up.

After the surgery, he hadn't stopped shooting up. He'd just started shooting into the sturdy sheep vein. It was stronger than his own diseased, collapsed veins, so he was able to keep using as he pleased. Hence the name, Sheepvein. Carla doesn't remember what his name was before that.

2

She suddenly sees a picture she needs to take. Red has leaned one arm up against the stucco wall above her head. The unzipped sleeve of his black leather jacket falls open, exposing his strong, root-like veins, branching up his arm, disappearing into the leathery shadows there. She picks up her camera with both hands. "Hold still, Red. Stay right there." She snaps the shot, adjusts the f-stop and shoots again. Red watches, amused. She has a portfolio of his body parts. Everyone who knows him knows that it's him, even though she's never shown his face. Many assume they're a couple, though that's just not right.

Red loves this little gal like a sister, which is why he calls her that. He would never, he thinks, think of crossing that line. Besides, from his experience, sex fucks things up. As long as he stays friends with Carla, she'll always be around. If they slept together, that would be the beginning of the end of it.

Carla rests her camera against her shirt, checking to see that the lens cap is still attached by its' cord to the camera itself. "Okay, thanks. You can move now."

Red pushes off from the wall. "Alright Miz Rock of Carla, where to next?"

Carla laughs and lightly punches Red's arm. She looks up the street, then back down the way they'd just walked. "I... don't know. Let's h'cup!" She opens her eyes wide at Red. "Oh no. H'cup!" She spits her gum out into the street. "Oh shit, Red, I can't stop hiccupping if I'm h'cup! High. And I can't hold my camera steady...H'cup!"

Red laughs. "You don't know how to stop them?"

Carla shakes her head and hiccups again. They come on fast and strong. She worries she may have trouble breathing. That happens when she hiccups while high.

"Okay. Let me try something. My grandma used to have us do this when I was a kid, and it's always worked for me." He reaches for her hands. "You'll have to stand in front of me and bend over. It's gonna look weird but trust me. This works."

Carla shuffles over to stand in front of Red and hiccups again. It hurts her chest each time, like something is seizing her from the inside and won't let go. She'll try anything, no matter how weird it looks. Red turns her around so that she is facing away from him. He places her hands on her waist and pushes on them slightly, forcing her to bend over. She looks over her shoulder up at him, and he nods. "Yup, you have to bend over, all the way. Don't lock your knees." She bends, forcing her head down to her knees, holding onto her camera with one hand. She was a dancer in school, and still limbers up, especially when she gets high. Her nose brushes against her bare knees, and a buzzing starts in her ears.

Red bends slightly too, so he speaks towards her tangle of crisp white hair. "I'm going to put my hands above your stomach, right below your chest. Okay? You take three big breaths, deep ones. All the way in and out. And on the third one, I want you to make sure to push all the air out. I'm going to push down then, and those hiccups will be gone."

Two men walk by, adorned with bushy handlebar mustaches and shiny cowboy boots. They laugh at Red and Carla, and lewdly urge him on. Carla hiccups. Red ignores them and says, "You ready?" She nods. She breathes in deeply, then out. H'cup. In, and out. In and hold... h'cup! And out. Tiny dark spots dance at the edge of her vision. Red clasps his hands more tightly around her abdomen and squeezes. The dark spots turn into wavy lines, and then she blacks out.

She wakes up lying loose-limbed on the hot, gritty sidewalk. Red is crouching by her side, and with one arm behind her back, is lifting her into a sitting position. There's a taste of blood in her mouth as Carla allows her vision to clear. Red's face at first is slightly hazy, out of focus, then it brightens, and she concentrates on his worried mouth. "What...?" She touches her camera, it seems to be fine. She raises her other hand to her lips and comes away with a brief smear of blood. "What the hell...?"

Red keeps his arm warmly around her shoulders for support. "You fainted. I must have squeezed too hard. I'm not used to doing that with someone so tiny. You're *small* lil sister... I think you're ok. You busted your lip. But your teeth look fine. Here, smile." He inspects her teeth. "Yeah, ok, cool, and you held onto that camera like nobody's business. So I think you're all fine other than that busted lip."

Carla touches her lip again and runs her tongue over her teeth. They seem fine. She holds her camera up again and looks it over carefully. It looks alright. She wipes her lip on the back of her tux sleeve, blotting a bright streak of blood onto the thin material. So much for this shirt. She wriggles her way out of Red's arms, and crouches onto the balls of her feet. She's uncertain about standing up quite yet. The buzzing in her ears is gone, and her vision is clear, but she worries about standing too quickly.

And hey, the hiccups are gone. She looks at Red. "It works! My hiccups are gone!"

He runs a hand over the sharp stubble on his chin. "Yeah...

it's not exactly supposed to work like *that*. I'm so sorry..."
He looks into her eyes and glances down at her lip. He turns
away. "I think that did me in. Scared the shit out of me, I
tell you."

Carla smiles and stands, resting one hand on Red's heavy
leather sleeve. Her teeth are stained with blood.

"Gross. You might want to rinse your mouth out." He spots
her drink, still standing where she'd placed it before she
fainted. He grabs it and hands it to her. "Here. Swish some
of this around and spit, I guess." She does. Her lip has
begun to swell slightly, so the bottle feels oddly small
against her mouth. "That was cool, even if you did drop me.
Thanks. Hey, take a picture of my lip, ok?"

She hands him the camera, turning the lens adjustments
in place first, and points where she wants him to focus
his attention. Red backs up, then moves closer again. His
hands are so huge around the camera. Carla wonders why
he doesn't play an instrument, bass maybe, or piano. She
places the tip of her tongue to the corner of her mouth,
and Red snaps two shots, click, whirr, click, whirr. She
grins, ouch, that hurts, and holds her hand out for
the camera.

"Thanks."

Two black men in worn grey suits walk up to the pair. They both wear somber ties and white hankies in their breast pockets. Carla thinks how she would love to take their picture, but something holds her back. She smiles at them. They ignore her and focus all their attention on Red. One of them flashes a fist in greeting.

"Hey brother. We're here on a mission." He looks to his friend. "We're here to set you right." His friend moves around Carla and steps in between where she and Red are standing, forcing her to step back. She furrows her brow slightly and tries to see around the intruder to where Red is now partly hidden from her view. Red steps to the side so he can see her too.

"Hey man. What's with pushing the lady out of the way? Not cool." His voice has deepened and taken on that menacing edge Carla recognizes from Red's protective persona on the street. She steps around, behind Red, and points the camera at the two men. Shoulder shot, snap.

One of the men is carrying a handful of leaflets. He picks one off the top and hands it across the short span of sidewalk between them to Red. "This here, brother, is what we're talking about. You sullying yourself, wasting your time, when there are sisters out here in need of a man such as yourself. They need for you to step up and take back what's yours, what's ours, and join us. Help us make this a strong nation, for the black man, once and for all."

Red glances at the pamphlet and hands it back to the man. "No way man. I'm not into this shit. Sorry, I'm a black man, that's true. But I'm also a red man, and a white man. I don't see the need to differentiate, to divide. And this..." He gestures at the pamphlets, "This is bullshit. You're never gonna get this to happen, and there's no reason to. Man, you're carrying the wrong message, *brothers*."

Carla steps away again, putting more space between her camera and what is happening here. She tries to get a better look at the pamphlets, but the man's hand covers most of what she can see. All she is able to make out is a portion of a U.S. map with a dotted line drawn horizontally across the middle. She moves around behind the light pole, and leans into its' rough, warm pocked surface. Its soft splintery bits feel welcoming against her bare leg and barely covered hip.

The two men step closer to Red. One of them places a hand on Red's shoulder, which he shrugs off. "Don't touch me. Man. I'm seriously not into this crap."

The men look at one another and back at Red. One of them says, "Your loss, brother of mine. Our loss too. But when this comes to fruition, you'll come to us and ask to be allowed in. Then we'll see what's *crap* and what isn't." He looks over at Carla when he says 'crap'.

Red lowers both arms and stands a little taller. He steps back, towards Carla. "Time for you to leave, gentlemen. Me and my friend have someplace to be." He cocks his head back towards Carla. She steps forward again and speaks up.

"What is this, anyway? What are you guys trying to sell him?" Red turns and shakes his head no at her, his eyes narrowed in warning. "That's alright lil' sister. I got this." Carla holds onto her camera with both hands nervously. She runs her tongue over her split lip and clamps her teeth together hard.

One of the men grimaces. "That's what we're talking about, brother. You have no business walking out with this *white* woman, when there's sisters who are more worthy... more desirable. I'm sorry," he places one hand over his shaded eyes. "You'll see. One day, you'll see." He turns to his friend, holding the pamphlets reverently with both hands, before him. "Come on Lazarus, let's leave this poor man to his fate. We'll see him down the road soon enough." They turn together and walk away, done here.

Red throws one fist up in the air after them. "Bullshit! What you two are preaching is bullshit!" He turns around and faces Carla. "Man…" He steps towards her, holding out both hands in a sort of peace offering, palms up.

Carla plants both of her feet in a wide stance, locking her knees and yells at the men as they walk away, "You fuckers! You don't know anything! Who the fuck do you think you are? Coming up to us, we're minding our own business, and you just waltz up and start fucking with my friend…"

One of the men stops. He reaches out and stops his friend. He turns slowly and levels a cold stare in her direction. His eyes are two crystal points of hate. He raises one arm like a lever and points at her. "YOU. Are the bullshit here. This *is* our business. He's a black man, and he belongs with us. Not you."

He stares her down, and Carla stares right back. The roof of her mouth has gone dry again. She smells a sudden sharp scent of something, fear? And tiny droplets of sweat trickle down her thin ribcage. Her shirt sticks to her skin. Oh, she's pissed now. This man, these men, their suits, their talk. She's still not quite sure what's going on, but she knows it's upset Red and they're putting her down and that pisses her off.

Red steps forward and holds both hands up, trying to decompress the situation. He speaks up, throwing his words at the two men. "Man, I'm telling you. Malcolm never preached this kind of hate. Not when he had his right mind." He reaches out and touches Carla on the shoulder. "Carla. Let's move."

A crowd has gathered at the edges of the sidewalk. Faces, feigning disinterest, laced with the lure of free entertainment, clot the street. Carla half-closes her eyes and looks down at her knees. She looks back up, at the two men walking away. She turns to the crowd.

"Just like a fucking circus. Hey! Lookit the animals and clowns! Oo oo oo!" She scratches at the top of her head with one hand and at her ribcage with the other. She jumps up and, turning her body to one side, trails one hand beneath her, loosely towards the sidewalk. A few of the crowd shuffle and turn away. Most make eye contact with a friend and wait for what Carla will do next.

She stops when she sees Red standing back away from her, arms crossed patiently, his mouth turned down in a grimace of hurt. She turns around and places a hand on his shoulder, where one of the men had touched him. "Yeah, ok. Let's go." Carla bares her teeth at the crowd, and refocuses on Red. She points up the street where the two men walked off. "What the hell was *that* all about?"

Red turns his head and spits into the street. A few of the

crowd closer in pipe up, "Hey, watchit..." Carla and Red ignore them now.

He looks down the street after the two receding men, and back at Carla. He sighs. "There's this thing, this movement, going on, where brothers and sisters- black folk- have been working to try to get this country split in two. Did you see the pamphlet?" Carla nods her head yes.

"Sort of. That's what that map was about? Splitting the country in two? Um... why?"

Red shrugs. "What these folks want is a nation split in two, with white folks on one side of the line, and black folks on the other."

Carla gasps. "*Really*?!" She raises both hands as though to hold off what he has just told her. Red shakes his head slowly, from side to side. He steers her away from the crowd. Some have moved closer to listen in. Red cuts them off with a look, and he and Carla walk slowly around the corner, acutely aware of one another and the crowd behind them. Red nods his head briskly once they are out of earshot of all those people.

"Yeah, really. I don't believe in it. I don't like it. I think it's just more bullshit to separate us from each other, instead of working to bring us together. It's a waste of time and effort. These... people could be working on so many other good things. For the community. For kids. For education, and art in schools, meals, afterschool care... shit like that." Red stops and smiles. "I sound like a goddamn preacher." He shakes his head, trying to dislodge thoughts of what just happened out of his mind. He leans against a light pole, his eyes following two men who walk past them, arm in arm.

"Man, ok, that did it. I'm done. Do you mind if I crash at your place?"

Carla snaps the lens cover off and focuses in on Red's jacket, creased and reflective in the glare of the unusual bright sunlight. She cocks one hip and cradles the camera against her face. Click, whirr, click, whirr. She answers as she peers through the viewfinder. "Of course you can crash at my place."

She rolls her eyes. "Ok, maybe I'm done for the night too. I mean day. For the week." She pauses and snaps the lens cap back in place. "Except for... I'm still high. There's no way I could sleep. I've got that, you know, brain fog thing going on but I'm still buzzin'..."

Red nods his head once in agreement. "Yup, I know what

you mean. For me, it's like there's a storm in my head. But hey, different weather systems, makes sense to me." He grins. Carla holds onto her camera with both hands and turns her head to one side.

"You know, I have a question about those guys. So... they thought that we were some white girl with her black boy? That sort of thing?"

Red grimaces. "Uh... yeah. Something like that."

Carla keeps her face turned to the side. She shakes her head in disbelief. "Like we would ever. They have no idea..."

Red reaches into his jacket pocket and pulls out another cigarette. He pushes off from the light pole, dragging hard on the moist tobacco as he lights up. "Low minds think low thoughts." He clamps the cigarette between his teeth and rolls it to one side of his mouth. He speaks through his gritted teeth. "It's like those new skins that have started to show up around town. They hate black people- they hate *me*- just for the color of our skin. Those men were only interested in me for the color of my skin. And in you for the color of yours, really. There's no humanity in any of that. There's just... hate. Without reason."

Carla sighs. "Without any *good* reason, that is."

Red nods. "Yeah, that's what I mean. So that's why I shave my head. Did you know that?"

Carla pushes her lower lip out, and shrugs. Red continues, "So people can see it's not the color of your skin that makes you a skinhead. It's the way you live. It's a choice, loving the music and the life, not who you're born being."

Carla waves a hand towards the street. "Let's get walking." She steps back. "Huh. I never thought about that. I mean, there's Buck the Fuck, and then there's you. It never crossed my mind you're both skins, but you're both so different."

Red starts off in the direction she has indicated. "Yeah, exactly. Luckily, there are more of us who are decent enough. You know, the guys in The Shits are good skins, for the most part. A bunch of their fans, that whole food bank scene, all those skins are good, mindful punks." He's talking about the assortment of skinheads who go to the Haight food bank. A number of them volunteer at the food bank and shelter. They follow political convictions with action, something Red approves of.

Carla smiles shyly to herself at his mention of The Shits. She flashes on Gabe's lips, his hands, the hard muscle of his arms, and feels a clench between her thighs. She takes a deep breath as they walk along, side by side. She looks over at Red. "It'll be nice, actually, to hang with you at my place. You can have some of this new chrysanthemum tea I just got, and crash, and I'll just take pics, if that won't bother you. I've got this new idea about photos from my balcony down at the street... Anyway, it'll be more peaceful. Not chaotic like out here..." She pushes her lower lip out again, feeling the split against her teeth. Red reaches out and brushes one hand against the wall to their right. They're walking away from her place, but around the block, away from the crowd back there on Polk. They'll turn up ahead and start back towards North Beach at the end of the street.

Carla brings the camera to her face and snaps a shot, here and there, of images only she notices, shadows, lines, and movement all around them. "I spy..."

"If you're alive, you can't be bored in San Francisco. If you're not alive, San Francisco will bring you to life."
– William Saroyan

Deep City Dive

1

Val rubs a hand over the stubble across the top and back of her head. Damn, she needs a shave, but there's no time. She pokes the toe of her steel-toed boot at the pile of clothes on the floor. I know there's a wool cap in here somewhere... there! She grabs the black wool watchman's cap and pulls it down over her ears, then pauses and looks around her small room. What else does she need before she heads out into the foggy wet night? She has her German army rucksack. As much as it weighs, she likes the pack. She has a few dollars from panhandling the other day- that was fun, telling folks she was a musician and needed the money to buy a reed for her horn. Hat, jacket, gloves, check, check, and check. She's good to go.

Val closes her bedroom door behind her and clips the combination lock onto the lockbar she installed a few months back. Someone- she has an idea who- kept breaking into her room and stealing drugs, money, even a few pieces of her crappy but beloved yard sale jewelry. So up the lockbar went, and now, every time she leaves the apartment, she locks her room up nice and safe.

She peeks into the back kitchen to see if anyone of interest is there. Sometimes Amy and Max are hanging out, shooting the shit. Sometimes Pat and one of her Rastafari gents are smoking and doing whatever it is exactly they do together. Henry used to hang with his dog on the back porch, when he was with Amy, but now the dog isn't allowed in the apartment, and besides, Henry has other fish to fry.

Nope, no-one there. Val clomps down the front stairs and out onto the street. There is a light drizzle of fog that feels good, refreshing even. Val lifts her face and greets the fog with closed eyes and a small smile. The drizzle will sort of fuck things up a little. It's harder to climb in and out of the bins safely when things are wet. But no matter. At least it's not raining. That would force the whole night to be called off.

Val ambles along the sidewalk in no great hurry. She has many blocks to walk, and plenty of time to get there. She figures she'll walk down Fulton, make her way over to Golden Gate, go through the Tenderloin, and see if there are any fags she can fuck with. Fun night!

She's looking forward to seeing her friend Kelly-Belly. They keep missing each other at shows or out and about in

The City. Kelly doesn't really spend much time outside the squat where she lives with a few other punks anymore. She used to always be on the scene when she lived in the Vats. Back then, she shared a tank with five other punkettes from around The City. Kelly had decorated her small corner of the tank with cobbled-together shelves, recycled garbage bag curtains, and an enormous assortment of plastic toys she'd pulled from various dumpsters around town.

That had been fun for a while. There were always bands rehearsing, and some nights, someone would build a fire and roast wienies, or people would just drift from vat to vat, seeing who was around, who had drugs, who wanted to hang out. But a few months ago, things had started to get strange. Someone was going around lighting fires just to see things burn. The cops and SFFD had been by more times than you could count on one hand, and that was too many times to have run-ins with the cops if you were a Vat Rat. Then Jimmy the Elf got sick- or was it his mom? Val couldn't quite recall. And then there were all those break-ins, people's things being rifled through and ripped off. A vigilante group had started up, and a couple of fuckheads who didn't even live at the Vats got busted for snooping around. The break-ins stopped after that, but still, things had gotten weird, and no-one really felt like there was a community there anymore, so Kelly packed up and moved into a squat over on Fulton, where she set up a bedroll and all her plastic toys in the closet she lives in there.

Kelly is absolutely one of Val's favorite people anywhere anytime. She is goofy and unique- not a copy-kitty like so many other punkettes out on the streets these days. She always has a smile, no matter what craziness is going on around her, and she's always game for some new adventure. Plus, she's no dummy. She may come across that way, at times, but the semi-vacuous front is just that- a mask to cover all the fun stuff going on deeper inside. Val likes to watch and listen to what Kelly comes up with next.

Val had stopped by the squat last week and spent half the night shooting speed and catching up with her old pal. Funny, she recalls, when Kelly had reacted to the small grey stuffed bunny Val had pinned to the front of her jacket, like a bouquet. One of its eyes had come loose and was dangling precariously, wobbling this way and that. Kelly had shrieked when she saw the rabbit. Val thought because Kelly had such a strong penchant for funky odds-n-ends like that. But no, it was weirder than Val could have imagined. Kelly grabbed Val's hand and led her through the dingy, dark apartment- they hadn't cut the lock on the electricity box yet, so they had no juice for lights.

Val tripped over some debris in the front room- it was so dark, she really couldn't tell what it was. Trash? A person?

She held onto Kelly's hand and let her lead the way. They got to the small closet where Kelly was crashing these days. It had a door, and the same kind of lock set up Val had on her door, which she approved of, bien fait. Kelly reached inside the closet doorway and picked up a dirty yellow flashlight. She had to shake it once or twice to get it to turn on, but then voila, let there be light! She pulled off her boots, and placing them inside the doorway, stepped inside.

"Come in! Don't worry about your boots. I'll scrunch up my sleeping bag." Kelly shoved her sleeping bag and the spongy egg carton foam she had stacked up beneath it as a mattress towards the back of the tiny room. At least it was a room, and she didn't have to share it with anyone else. She'd strung all her plastic toys from one side of the ceiling to the next, crisscrossed dozens of times to create a sky of toys above her. Sleeves of tinsel shimmered along the two walls on either side of the bed, and someone had spray-painted obscenities and the names of some bands on the far wall, which sometimes mysteriously felt sticky and wet. At the foot, just inside the door, Kelly had put up shelves to hold some clothes, a few books, and a store of candles, jello boxes, and shiny things Kelly liked to collect off the streets.

Val shuffled into the room, not wanting to step on anything precious to her friend, she had so little these days to hang onto. She leaned against the closet doorframe and looked around. The closet was pretty damned tiny, but this was a better situation than Kelly had had at the end there, out at the Vats. She nodded, "This is cool. I like it. And you don't have to worry about sharing a bathroom with 50 people!"

Kelly laughed. "Which never worked anyway!"

She grabbed both of Val's hands in hers, and said, "Ok, are you ready for this?" She touched the rabbit on Val's jacket and reached onto one of the lower shelves at the foot of her bed. When she withdrew her hand from the recess of the shelf, she held up another grey bunny rabbit. *Exactly* like the one pinned to Val's jacket.

"I mean... what the fuck?!" Val exclaimed. "That is.. that is the *exact* same bunny!" She reached out to take it from Kelly's hands, and turned it over a few times, careful not to dislodge the one button eye, hanging loosely by a few remaining threads in its socket. "Did you *see*?!" She pointed at her own rabbit's dangling eye and snorted.

"That's crazy!! I know! Where did you get that?"

"I don't remember exactly. I was dumpster diving last week over off of Haight, up in the Aves, really. I found it somewhere up there." She handed the second rabbit back to Kelly. "So what's your story, then, little fella? Where did you come from?"

Kelly shook her head, "No way. No *way*. I was dumpster diving downtown. You know how I like to hit the trash bins all around the big stores down there. People throw out some amazing things– shit that only has a small cut or tear or ding in it. Larry and I had hooked up and were making our rounds. He was hoping to find wigs, for some reason. He has this crazy idea about some kind of hair shirt thing he's going to do next." She laughed again. "But yeah, I found this bunny– *just like this*– with the eye dangling off it and everything!"

Kelly sat on the end of her bedroll. "How insane is that? That we would each find the exact same stuffed rabbit at opposite sides of The City on the same night?"

Val snorted this time. "Unfuckingbelievable. That's got to be some kind of... I don't know. Like it was meant to be? A little spooky too, if you ask me. Magic stuff, oooo..."

Kelly placed the rabbit on her lap, while she fiddled with its eye. She pointed to a pile of fabric on one of the shelves. "I also found all this great fabric. I'm going to make curtains for the house, and for my door, so when I'm home, I can leave the door open and still have some privacy. It gets hot with the door closed, and it's gross, and this wall back here sort of leaks if the door is shut." She reached back and ran her finger along the back wall. She showed her finger to Val. It was wet, which couldn't be good.

The two friends had then settled in for the night. Val had originally stopped by hoping to find Kelly to share the new batch of speed she'd picked up earlier that evening from Annie-X. They got high, sharing Kelly's dull needle, and spent the rest of the night spinning stories, and drinking the warm beers Kelly had stashed under her bed.

Sometime before dawn, when Val really *really* needed a cigarette, she decided to head out, so they'd made plans to meet tonight, and hit these famed dumpsters Kelly and Larry were always going on about.

Val nearly skips through the streets, steaming her way across Van Ness into the Tenderloin. She's feeling pretty high right about now, and always enjoys a good chuckle by scaring some local faggot turning tricks on Polk. She turns left off of Golden Gate, past the big government-looking buildings and towards the lively, brightly lit rows of shops and bars further up in the Gulch.

Val likes flashing by the windows as she trips along,

imagining owning this thing or that arrayed in each shop, in her own imaginary little Colorform world. Sometimes, she creates a whole new self, and fills an apartment, a house, with the things she chooses from each window display. Not tonight though. Tonight, she's on a mission. Get to the dumpsters out behind Macy's where she and Kelly have planned to meet up and get down to some serious pro-*fess*-ional dumpster diving. And find some fag to torment for a few minutes, along the way, just to spike her high a little bit.

She's anxious to get to the fun stuff, so she picks up her pace, nearly marching down the length of each block. Not here, where there are more apartment buildings. She barely notices the brick facades, the stairwells and gleaming doorways she hustles past to get up the road to where she knows the action is. Past Geary, then Post, and ahhh, now she can start to look for signs of the native faggot. She is the great white huntress, and she will stalk and take down her prey.

Val knows- more or less- which corners hold the largest groups of little fag-boys, all eye-shadowed and glittered up for sale. She still has a few blocks to go until she reaches the corners nearest the Cinch and all those hustler bars. But still, she's keeping her eyes peeled, left and right. She doesn't want to go too far and have to double back to get to Union

Square. She hopes Kelly shows up alone, she realizes. As fun as Larry the Lush can be, he's still another fag, and Val would rather not have to share her friend's attention. They always seem to have so much better adventures when it's just the two of them deciding where to go and what to do next.

There! In front of that funky little leather shop, where Val bought the small leather and chain cockring she's wearing around one thin wrist, there's a perfect specimen. The slender, glammy boy-toy leaning against the light post, pretending to care about the cigarette he's limply holding in one hand is perfect game. He's predictably all decked out in glittery gold short shorts, a rainbow tube top for fuck's sake, and half-feathered, half-rooster crown hair. Val checks him out and shakes her head derisively. He doesn't even have a package, why would he wear such tight shorts if there's nothing there to even display?! Ew, either way.

Val crosses the street and slips between the two cars parked behind her target. She pauses and checks to make sure there isn't anyone else lurking nearby. Just another fairy on the opposite corner, wearing pink gauzy wings and carrying a furry purse. Val takes a deep breath, then steps up to the young man. She jabs him on the shoulder with two fingers, "Hey, Faggot!"

He inhales quickly and spins around, "Don't!! What?!"

Holding his cigarette out in front of him like a weapon, the boy immediately recognizes Val's intent. He knows the stories well, though he's been lucky enough so far in his time on the streets to have avoided any run-ins with hateful, angry fag-bashers. "Sister, you can Just. Back. Off." He thrusts his cigarette at Val in a stabbing motion and moves away from her, towards the corner.

"Excuse me?" Val cups a hand to her ear. "Did I just hear you threaten me? You little fairy?!" She grins hard, oh this is fun. "And I am No. Sister. Of. Yours."

The boy glances around quickly. Is there anyone who can help him out here? Should he scream for help? Will anyone come? He too sees the mustached fairy princess across the way, but sh/he doesn't seem to notice, and across the street is too far, if something bad happens. Something worse than this. He looks back at Val, through long, curled eyelashes.

"Bah! You fucking make me *sick*!" She cries, and raising both arms into the air, Val shapes her hands into claws and charges the fag. "GAAAAAAHHHHH!!!!!" He screams, light and shrill, surprised more than scared at first. Is this really happening? Then quickly he sees what's happening for what it really is. Val isn't really attacking him. She has no weapon, no gun or knife. She's just messing with him. Trying to scare him and make him look weak and foolish.

"You BITCH!" He screams at her. He plants his skinny legs and with both hands in fists at his sides, leans back towards her. "You are a *hor*rible, *stu*pid, *aw*ful little person!!"

Val stops mock-attacking the boy, and starts laughing so hard she has to grab her stomach. Oh! She never thought one of them would actually have the spitfire and *balls* to fight back! This is just perfect. Val feels the rush of the game and enjoys it. There's that flush, almost like right after the drugs first wash through your bloodstream. Whew! Well then, that's what she came for. She cocks both forefingers at the boy and click click shoots him with her hands. He screams again, more *at* her this time than in surprise. "Go a*way*!" So she does.

Val backs up with both hands in the air. Ok, you win... As she slips between both cars and back onto the street, she turns and grins at the boy. "That was kinda fun, donchya think?"

He takes a step towards her, "No! I don't think that at ALL! I hope you DIE!"

Val laughs so hard she nearly pees herself. She grabs her crotch and holds on tight. The boy sees this and thinks she's making fun of him again. "Oh *you* make *me* sick! What is *wrong* with you people?!" Then realizing he has just provoked his aggressor, the boy looks both ways and runs across the street to the fairy princess there. Save me!

Val just makes it across the street before she has to crouch down to stop herself from peeing. Stop. Laughing! She wishes Sophie had been here to see this. Thinking of her friend sobers her up slightly. Oh shit, she's got to get going before she makes Kelly wait too long. She doesn't think this took all that long, but time tends to fly in crazy circles when you're high, so... Val straightens up and checks with one hand to make sure she hasn't actually wet herself. Nope.

Heading back down Polk, she turns left at Bush and heads for the Square. If she beats the lights, she'll make it in no time. But just as she reaches the first massive buildings that make up Union Square, she smacks herself on the forehead with one open palm. "Oh *merde*!! Kelly didn't say *Union* Square. She said *Embarcadero Center*!" Fuck fuck fuck. Ok, it's ok. She breaks into a quick jog and trots past the multiple blocks of Union Square. Turning left on Battery, she feints around the block, back up Sacramento, and running at a pretty steady clip now, loses herself momentarily in the glittery bright lights that line the streets and building entrance.

Now Val is wracking her brain, trying to remember where Kelly said they should meet, exactly. She stands there with her hands on her hips just a second, before deciding what to do. Her mind is racing with the speed, the bright lights, the fun she had with the boy back there on Polk, and now... she spins on her toe to the right and starts walking that direction. She'll walk around the perimeter of the building and find Kelly that way.

She reaches the corner, turns left, and aims for the alleyway towards the end of the street. She's *pretty* sure that's where Kelly had said they should meet up. Val knows she's late now too, so she picks up her pace and jogs a bit until she reaches the alley. Left again, and there she is, whew. Hanging off the side of a pair of dumpsters, looking like she already has a little stash of goodies piled up at her feet.

2

Val hollers out "Woop!" and she slows down to her regular loping walk, no need to hurry now. They've got aaaaall night. Kelly is half-in half-out of the dumpster, legs kicking and trying to keep a toe-hold as she stirs through whatever treats fill the waste bin. She plants her feet on the lip halfway up the side of the bin, and pulling herself up to rest on her hands, looks over at Val with a crazy happy grin on her face. "This is a goldmine! Get over here. You're not going to believe what they threw away!"

Val trots over, drops her rucksack on the ground next to Kelly's small pile of treasure, and pulls her gloves out of her jacket pockets. She peers over the edge of the dumpster into the mysteries that await her while she pulls on her gloves, then grabs ahold of the rim and hoists herself up, clambering over and in. She lands on a short stack of flattened shirt boxes, empty, but torn. The contents of the dumpster are fairly dry. Kelly must have muscled the lids open before monkeying around inside. Val points to one end of the dumpster and then back to where Kelly was leaning half in to begin with. "Shall I...?" Kelly says "I haven't got to that end yet. I just started here. I was waiting for you to get here before we really dove all in, as it were" Her eyes sparkle, yup, she's high as a kite too.

Val steps carefully around the pile Kelly seemed to be rummaging through, and starts picking through the jumble of boxes, fabric, and large paper bags, filled with presents just waiting to be opened. There seem to be a lot of fancy dress shirts, frilly skirts and blouses, clothes she couldn't care less about. But she keeps picking. The deeper you dig, the tastier the treasure once found. Ah! She wraps her fingers around a thick wool something or other and pulls it free. It's a gorgeous wool short-waisted sweater, grey so dark it's nearly black. Turning it over, Val sees why it's been thrown away. There are 3 long jagged slashes across the back, like someone attacked the sweater with a really large fork. Perfect. She holds the sweater up for Val to see, who whistles appreciatively, then she tucks it into her belt and turns back to the pile.

She doesn't find anything else of interest there. If only some of the fancy blouses had been larger sizes, she would have grabbed them for Annie-X. She kick-nudges the pile of sorted boxes and bags to the rear of the dumpster, clearing a path to the other end, and heads first to what seems to be a box of electronics. Maybe something good...

They poke around the pair of dumpsters for most of an hour, sort through their finds, pack them up and move on. Val had grabbed two aqua-marine plastic transistor radios that had been dumped by the boxload along with everything else in the bin. She hopes she can get them to work. If they do, she plans to set them up at opposite corners of her room for a stereo affect, listening to a couple of the pretty good radio shows she likes.

Kelly had grabbed handfuls of the flouncy blouses that Val had rejected. She plans to cut them up and re-sew them into diaphanous curtains she can hang around the squat for texture. It's always nice to have something to space out on when your eyes start bugging out on speed. Kelly imagines windows open, these curtains billowing softly in any kind of cross breeze, one of her favorite records playing softly from the next room. Once they get the electricity on.

They walk around the outside of the complex, and arrive back at the entrance, with all its shimmering bright lights and looping staircases. Val pops a smoke from the pack in her front shirt pocket and lights up. She looks to Kelly inquisitively. Do we go up? Val's never actually been to Embarcadero Center, though she's heard Kelly and Larry brag about their dumpster scores often enough. Kelly giggles, "Come on!" She starts up the stairs, her re-cycled shopping bag filled to the brim with blouses, colorful wooden peg games, and fancy chocolates. The chocolates were *fine*, just the corners of the boxes they were in had been dented or slit open.

They walk up the stairs, glancing out at the street in all its shining brightness. At the top, they reach a second level that allows them to walk back across the street bridge to whatever is on the other side or continue back into the belly of the building where Val wonders what they'll find next. Kelly beckons Val to follow her back down the stairs to the street level entrance. She has something she wants to show her.

At the base of the stairs, Kelly walks them around the stairwell along a narrow tiled walkway that leads them to a large rectangular fountain surrounded by shrubs and flowers. The fountain fills the room with the smell of chlorine and a soothing sound of trickling water. They walk up to the fountain and peer in. Huh, there are coins scattered all around the base of the fountain. But not enough that Val feels like taking her boots off or getting them wet. "Just you wait." Kelly says with a toothy smile. "Let's go this way." Val looks around her at the closed and shuttered shops that surround them. She figures it must be close to two in the morning. She hopes there's no security guards.

She shifts the rucksack on her shoulder. When the straps get wet, they get heavy and dig into her arms. She thinks about wrapping her new sweater around one of the straps for cushioning. Once they get to a place where she can do some field work, she'll check that out. Val follows Kelly up a straight flight of stairs that leads them to the second level. Kelly says "Not here, not yet," and trips up the next flight of stairs to the third level, leading them to the upper level of the fountain, where they can look straight back down two floors to the rectangular pool below.

And Val sees what Kelly meant. There are four narrow bridges that link the fountain to the floor she is standing on. Too narrow for anyone to safely walk upon; they must be ornamental, or structural somehow for the tall steel and cable artwork that decorates the fountain. Or is part of it. She looks more closely and sees that the water flows down and through pieces of the artwork, little waterfalls and rivulets bouncing off the gongs and cables that make it seem like some kind of science fiction elevator. Her eye is drawn back to the narrow bridge closest to her. For that's where the prize is; where the challenge and goodies lie in wait. Each bridge is completely covered with coins- big coinage too- not nickels and pennies like on the bottom floor.

Val realizes someone must clean out the main floor fountain so that punks like her- or kids, whoever- don't climb in and steal the change that 'normal' people throw in with their wishes. But there's no way they could get a cleaning crew to reach the money up here. She shrugs, that's because they're all wimps, and are afraid of the adventure. She looks over at Kelly, who is smiling hugely back at her. "Yup, see what I mean? Every time Larry and I come here, we walk up here to look around. There's another secret I'm going to show you next. But we always try to figure out– how can we get to that cash?"

Val gets it as soon as Kelly says it. Oh... *she's* brave enough– insane enough– to give it a try. And why the hell not? "Oh hell yes. I'm in." She plops down right there and starts to unlace her boots, then removes her gloves, and finishes pulling both boots off, stuffing her clean double stripe athletic socks inside each shaft. She pulls off her hat and shoves that into her jacket pocket, which she also removes and lays on the ground on top of her rucksack. There's a glass wall she has to climb over– easy enough– to get to the bridge. Val is light and limber. She easily hoists herself over the wall and lowers herself carefully, toes reaching for some kind of purchase, onto the pebbly bridge. Uh, she hopes it can hold her weight, even as light as she is.

Holding onto the glass wall with one hand, Val bends down and reaches into the bridge's trough, brimming with coins. She scoops up a handful of coins and realizes she doesn't have any place to put them. She turns to Kelly, who is nervously wondering what *she* should be doing. "Eh, Kelly... can you get me a bag or something?"

Kelly spins in place, quickly looking around for something Val can use. "Of course! Wait…" She runs over to a trash can parked against the wall and flips open the heavy lid. Perfect, the cleaning crew has already been here. She tears the heavy plastic trash bag off of the can and runs back to where Val is still hanging onto the glass wall with one hand. Kelly holds the bag open, and Val pours the coins in. They mostly clank to the bottom, but some stick to the sides. Kelly shakes the bag lightly, then folds the opening back over and over again until it becomes a roughly grocery bag-sized shape. "I'll hold it for you. Hurry up. This is really scary." Kelly holds the bag over the edge of the glass wall, so Val doesn't have to bend, scoop, stand, pour. She can simply bend, scoop, reach over and pour instead. Much better. Val reaches as far as her long arms will extend, holding on to the wall with one sweaty hand, and scooping up coins with the other.

Once she's cleaned out all the coins as far as she can reach, Val stands and tentatively takes a step out along the bridge. But no, she's sweating and shaking- both from the speed and the craziness of the thing she's daring herself to do. Her heart is beating loudly in her ears, thumping wildly in her chest. Nope nope nope. She quickly eases her foot back to the end of the bridge and holds onto the glass wall with both hands.

Kelly lets out a loud whoosh of air, as though she'd been holding her breathe. She starts to put the trash bag of booty down. "Can I help...?" Val shakes her head no. She just needs to have her heart slow down a bit, then she can climb back over the wall easily. She waits a few moments, then to hell with it. She hangs one leg over the wall and pushes off with the other leg, landing on one ass cheek. Kelly grabs her friend's arm and pulls her to safety as Val falls to the floor in an undignified heap.

She lies there a minute, heaving and sweating. Fuck, that was crazy! Val looks up at Kelly, "Ok, I'm ready. Let's do that again!" She jumps up to her feet, pauses, and reaches into her jacket pocket for one of her gloves. Then rolling her shoulders back, points to the trash bag and says, "Can you hold that again? I'm just going to stay close to the wall and get as much money as I can from there." She walks over to the next bridge span, around the corner from the first. There are four spokes, one at each midpoint of the square opening around the fountain.

At the next span, Val stops, taking a few deep breaths to try to slow her heart down a bit more. You can do this, she thinks to herself, then grabs onto the glass partition with both hands, and climbs over to the other side. Easy... This time, she hangs onto the wall with her gloved hand, and kneeling down, reaches out to scoop up as many coins as possible with her other. Scoop, reach back, drop into the trash bag that Kelly is holding as far over the ledge as she can. When she's scooped up all the coins she can reach, Val stands, stretches one long leg out, and pulls more coins towards her with her foot. Haha! She kneels again and scoops up all these new coins. So clever! So much fun! She wonders how much booty they're grabbing.

They move to the third and then fourth spans, raking in all the coins Val can reach. By the time she has finished and pulled herself back over the wall, she's stopped sweating, and her heart is beating normally- as normally as it does when just on speed, and not doing stupid stunts like she just pulled. Val drops to the ground, folds her legs up, and draping her arms over her knees, gestures to Kelly to come sit too. She does, placing the bag of loot between them.

They both peer into the bag, which has become quite heavy. Kelly is glad Val has her rucksack with her. That will make it easier to carry the cash out of here. Which reminds her. She stands and reaches out a hand for Val to grab so she can pull her up. "We should get going. It's probably about three? And I'm not sure, but I think cops patrol the Center every few hours."

That does it. Val grabs Kelly's offered hand and hoists herself up. She picks up the trash bag and feels her arms strain with the weight. "Wow, Kelly! You're strong. This got heavy..." She can hardly wait to get back to... wherever they're going after this- to count out their winnings. Probably Kelly's pad. Fewer people tend to hang out there, so they won't have to explain or share.

Kelly walks back to where their things are piled at the first bridge and picks up her shopping bags from the dumpster dive. "Can you carry the money in your backpack? I think it's too heavy for my bags." She holds them up so Val can see how flimsy they are.

"Oh sure. Can I put my sweater in one of your bags?" Val trots over and pulls her dumpster score out, handing it to her friend. Then she rolls the trash bag full of coins closed and shoves it, clinking, into her rucksack, latches the flap shut, and shoulders the pack squarely. "This is really heavy!" She starts to turn towards the stairs to head back the way they came, but Kelly grabs her arm.

"Nope, I have one more thing to show you. Let's go this way." Kelly gestures towards the walkway that crosses the street, linking the building they're in with another across the way. Val had noted the walkway but didn't really think about where it led.

Kelly notices Val's look of curiosity as they hoof it across the skybridge. "This is *all* Embarcadero Center," she explains and gestures from one building to the next. "I think it actually goes for something like four blocks around? There are hotels, and I think a convention center, or something. That's where we're going." As they reach the other side, they both turn back and see the large Hyatt Regency sign across the way.

"Oh ok, so the hotel is back there. Still..." Kelly turns around again and grabs Val's arm, pulling her past a group of planters with various sized trees and floral arrangements. She's in a hurry now, feeling the air shift to that pre-dawn calm before things get moving on the streets below.

They turn sharply past the planters and come upon two large counter height cabinets, pushed together to form a deep, tall table of sorts. Val has no idea what it might be. Then Kelly grabs one end of one of the cabinets and pulls it away from the other. They're on wheels or tracks of some kind, and the cabinet pulls back pretty easily, revealing shelves stocked with booze of every kind. Val whistles, then slaps her own hand over her mouth, oops, too loud. Her eyes wide, she grins at Kelly from behind her hand. "Let's grab another trash bag!"

As soon as she says this, Val spins away from Kelly and

runs over to a medium-sized, square-mouthed trash can behind the bar area. She flips the lid off, then makes a small moue with her mouth, damn, there's trash in this one. But wait, she pulls the bag aside and looks, and yes! Underneath it, there is a clean, folded trash liner. Val reaches in, grabs that, and shakes it open as she walks back over to Kelly, who is pulling bottles out from the shelves and placing them on top of the bar. Tequila, some enormous bottles of vodka, some kind of no-brand whiskey, and one of Val's personal faves, Cointreau. The bottle looks brand new, fantastique!

Kelly stops pulling bottles from the shelves and looks at the trash bag Val has handed her. "Oh shit, this isn't the good kind, the heavy kind. I think we can only put two or three bottles in this before it tears. Crap. I can put something in my bags. I think one more thing should be ok." She looks at Val and back at the liquor, pulling the smaller bottles away from the big bottle of vodka. Val helps her, loading the tequila and Cointreau into the bag she'd grabbed. It already tears a little in her hands, so she says, "That's all it can take. Shit. I wish we didn't have so much money in my rucksack!"

They both grin at one another, and as Kelly ponders between the vodka and whiskey, they see a small beam of light flash past them, along the wall, then across the bar.

They both duck, and the bottles clink as the bag Val is holding touches the ground. Shit! They look at each other wide-eyed and scared. Kelly shrugs, what do we do? Val looks around, and notices there are only two options that she can see: either go back the way they came, across the skybridge, or head over that way, to the stairs beyond the restaurant she now sees they're robbing. She nods her head in that direction.

Both girls crouch-walk around the end of the bar, Val hugging the bag of bottles close to her belly. She moves carefully, dragging one hand along the side of the bar to help keep her balance as she moves crab step by crab step forward. Kelly is carrying her two shopping bags, elbows lifted high in the air above her body as she tries not to make any noise. The circle of light flashes past them again, over their heads. They each hold their breath and pause, as they hear light footsteps walk towards them from the opposite corner of the open gallery.

Val guesses that if they make a run for it from here to the stairway, whoever is holding the flashlight across the way won't be able to see them. She looks into Kelly's eyes and nods slightly towards the stairs, then raises her body into a lesser crouch and walks quickly, quietly, to the stairwell. Kelly looks at the bags she's holding, decides, and leaves one by the end of the bar, then mimics Val and quickly, quietly, makes her way in a high crouch to the stairwell.

Once there, they both step as silently as they can, one, two, three... They can't hear anyone behind them, so they descend more quickly, and at the next level, break into a light-footed run, aiming for the narrow stairs that take them down one more level between two high walls and onto the street. Behind them, they can just hear someone yell out, "Hey! Who's there?!" So they hit the street, and bear left, running all out. At the end of the street, they turn the corner and pause. There's no one chasing them, and they take a second to figure out what to do, where to go next.

They have just run past a construction zone that started at the bottom of the stairs, with scaffolding and large sheets of plywood erected as a fence, surrounded by a barrier of bright orange weighted plastic barricades and yellow 'do not cross' tape. Val looks at the bag in her hands, shakes her head slightly from side to side, and places the bag and its' contents against the plywood wall. "Just in case they call the cops. I don't want to have incriminating evidence in my hands..."

Kelly nods and lifts the one bag she has in her hands as proof of the same thinking. "Yeah... I left the bag with those radios and shirts. I've got your sweater though!" She smiles brightly, then turns her face to the streetlight above them. "Ugh..."

The sky has just started to fade to a paler grey. It's morning, and *no* time to be stuck downtown. Kelly checks the street signs above them, and points with her free hand up Sacramento, towards Battery and home. Val pulls on her cap, and lights a cigarette as they walk proudly, each with a victorious spring in her step, away from the scene of such successful and fruitful dumpster dive. Val smirks around her cigarette and says, "That's what I call a deep city dive..." and the girls march up the street, squinting against the brightening day. They are both *so* ready to get back to the safety of Kelly's dark squat where they can count their cash, and then?

"I have always been rather better treated in San Francisco than I actually deserved."— **Mark Twain**

Get In The Van

1

The scratched white panel van careens around the corner, pulls a California stop at the street's dogleg turn, and rolls down the avenue, rocking slightly over the roughly patched cobbled pavement. Gabe leans into the steering wheel as he drives, feeling the hard rim of the wheel press against his lower ribs. He rests one hand on the transmission knob, an undersized eight-ball mounted on the end of the broken shaft. Layers of glue have dried around the base of the knob. Gabe flicks at the edges of glue with his thumbnail, in time to the music blaring over the van's trashed speakers.

At the light, he leans back into the body of the driver's seat. His sister bought the band one of those beaded seat covers that supposedly massages your back as you drive. Piece of shit doesn't work. But Gabe doesn't have the heart to tell her.

"California! Uber-alles! California! Uuuuuber-alles!" Gabe sings along, both flicking at the eight-ball glue with one hand and tapping on the steering wheel rim with the other. KUSF is playing some pretty good shit today. Afternoons, before practice, Gabe sometimes throws a cassette into this crappy little sea-foam green Sanyo radio cassette deck his mom bought him for Christmas last year and records a half hour of whatever show is on that's playing a good run of tunes. Today he taped The Ramones, Pavement, Lords of the New Church, The Dead Kennedys, and Rudimentary Peni. They even played some less well-known local Cali bands like Tragic Mulatto and Stukas Over Bedrock. Whenever there's crap on, one of KUSF's reggae programs or that new wave shit he can't stand, Gabe plugs one of his tapes into the deck and listens to his own private radio show over and over again.

He cruises down the street, momentarily forgetting which way to turn. Is Pat's to the left or right? Where the hell is he? Oh right, turn right at the freakin' purple house with the scary turrets there on Baker. Now look for parking... ah fuck it. He pulls over sharply and abruptly to a stop and punches the horn with the palms of both hands. He leans out the window and yells up to the second floor above him.

 "Hey! Max! Hobo!" He stabs at the horn again while leaning the upper half of his torso outside the van, over the car parked legally next to him on the street. "Let's go!" Hobo is Gabe's personal nickname for Henry. Ever since Henry left for Germany right out of high school, then returned last year, he's been a bit of a wanderer. Gabe admires that. The only place he's ever been is on tour up and down through California with the band. Other than that, he's a homebody. An Eastbay homebody. One of these days though, he'll jump a train with Hobo there and see something *real*.

Henry's shiny dome peeks out from the window in the apartment above where Gabe is double-parked. He waves absent-mindedly, almost more of a flutter than a salute. Gabe wonders about this guy sometimes. Hell, you can't spend four years in the army surrounded by a bunch of guys and not get into *something* off-color. Sophie peeks out over the window ledge, her short bang fringe sticking out in fingered spikes, a punk halo. Looked like she didn't even have a shirt on. So, the flutter thing, maybe not. He laughs at himself and snorts, nah. Henry is definitely one hetero-mother-fucker. Don't know about that little wave out the window though.

He hits the horn again, twice, and looks around the street to see if he's pissing anybody off. Nope, no one's really noticing. He looks up towards the bay window again when suddenly someone body slams into the side of the van.

"What the Fuh...?" Gabe jumps in his seat. He snaps his head to the right and sees Henry and Max hanging off the side-mirror, mugging at him. Max is making monkey faces and rolling his eyes up into his head. Henry is grimacing and getting his face to turn bright red. It's scary how he can do that. Something about how he forces pressure into his skull or something like that. He's explained it to Gabe before, but Gabe just couldn't figure it out. That's another special Hobo talent, evidently.

"Assholes." He laughs. "Get in the van. Time's a tickin'."

Henry pulls open the rusted passenger door and jumps in. "Shotgun!" Max lets go of the side-mirror and flips Henry off. "Fuck you, man... I always ride bitch." He walks around to the back of the van and opens one of the two double doors there. Stepping in, he grabs the hank of bright red frightwig they have fastened to the inside of the door as a handle, and pulls it shut behind him. Careful to step over ragged drum cases and Henry's olive-colored gig bag rolling around the floor, Max makes his way to the bottom-up milk crate leaning against the pitted bulkhead behind Gabe's chair. He sits down, folding his long legs into a defensive position. Time to hold on with whatever he's got.

Gabe turns around to look. "You all settled in there, Dude?" He smirks. They love to 'surf-talk' when it's just the two or three of them. Max flips Gabe off too, and grunts. "Yeah. I'm all good. *Dude*."

Henry smiles and hits the dash with his hand. "Let's go, man. We need to run through two sets and Larry needs to set up for The Lewd tonight."

Gabe salutes. "Yessir, Sarge sir!" calling Henry by his other nickname, one that suits his public persona well. Gabe turns the key, pops the clutch in, and lurches the van, jerking, down the street. Henry and Max rock in their seats violently, both grabbing onto whatever is nearby to stop from rolling around so hard. Max mutters, "Fuckin' chill, Dude." He braces himself with both feet planted hard into the blackened oily floor and reaches out to grasp at the driver's seat with one hand and the bass drum, shifting dangerously beside him, with the other.

Gabe's face creases in thought. "Wait a sec. The *Lewd's* playing tonight? Why didn't I know about that?"

Henry laughs. "I don't know, man." Gabe turns the radio down, some wanker shit with a bunch of electronic synthesizers. Henry adds, "Show's not at The Tool and Die. It's over in Berkeley."

Max pipes up. "No, that's next week, Dude. That big festival thing is next week."

Henry shifts sideways in his seat so he can see Max hanging

on, then looks up at Gabe. "Yeah man. You know about this. We tried to get in on the show, but it's all LA bands and a couple other bands from up north and around. The Lewd, T.S.O.L., DOA, 7 Seconds... um, The Fix." He pauses and thinks. "Where those guys from?"

Gabe answers, "They're from England, right? What the fuck? I mean, now I remember, but I thought that was supposed to be an American punk fest?"

Henry shakes his head, no. "No man. That's The Fixx you're thinking of- with two 'X's. They suck raw cock. All fucking new romantic bullshit. Nah, The Fix is on Touch-n-Go. They're from Mississippi or... no, Michigan. You've heard 'em."

Max leans forward between the two front seats to hear better and be heard. "Oh yeah... Amy's got their 'Vengeance'. That's a great fucking tune, man."

Gabe smashes his fist onto the dashboard above the radio. "What the FUCK? We still shoulda had the gig. What the fuck are they doing bringing in bands from Michigan or wherever when we live right here?" He licks his lips and presses them together. "Who do we have to talk to?"

Max pushes himself back against the bulkhead and closes

his eyes. Henry holds both hands out in a calming gesture. "Whoa, man. You sound like *me*. You've known about this festival, you said, right? It's over in Berkeley by the train tracks, some water park or something. It's been set up for a long time. All those Re-Search guys are doing something out there. A bunch of these bands just happened to be on tour and it just came together. It's gonna be a great fucking show. I hear the Angels are gonna be there, running security. So we gotta be cool, man. But what a great line-up. And Sophie says a bunch of the Clits and their friends are gonna do a wet t-shirt thing. That's worth heading across the Bay alone." He pauses. "And uh, hey, I hear Carla's shooting the whole thing. That should be cool." Henry narrows his eyes at Gabe. "Donchya think?"

Gabe snorts. He never should have told the guys about Carla. Nothing's happened since he got pistol-whipped. He wonders if she thinks he's a wuss for not fighting those assholes off better than he did. She seemed to be cool after it happened. Hell, he figured they'd have got together by now, the way she was flirting with him. But she hasn't been to any shows, and Shelly says she hasn't been around lately to buy. Gabe runs a hand over his jaw. Figures though. He's kinda skittish about hanging at Shelly's too, now. He can't blame Carla. Still... what the fuck is he supposed to do?

Max yelps as they round a corner and he braces himself

once again against instruments and debris rolling dangerously all around him. "Um... hey man. Take it easy. And... I think the Lewd's playing tonight at the Tool and Die, *and* next week in Berkeley. Isn't that why we have to clear out early?"

Henry looks down at his hands. "Yeah, I guess so." He leans across the dash and turns the radio up. "Speaking of..." The ragged, brash guitar of the Lewd's 'Kill Yourself' pipes out heavily yet still tinny from the van's dying speakers.

The three quiet down and muse in deference to the three-chord dementia scratching the empty space between them. Max plays air drums, making little 'schoo' sounds along with each plash of his hands. Henry presses his lips together and half closes his eyes. First time he heard these guys he was just about to head for home from Germany. That was nearly two years ago, and here they are, living it up large, doing the whole touring life. Man...

They turn onto Mission, and Gabe starts looking for parking a few blocks from the club. Mexican shops line the street, filling the air with pungent smells of hot spices and cooked beans, and the oompa of traditional Norteño music. Henry averts his gaze to avoid eye contact with a small group of Chicano teenage boys clumped together at the corner. The light won't change though, so he sneaks a look and finds them doing the same. One of them flashes a sign with the fingers of both hands at the van. Henry knows it's some kind of local gang thing, but he ignores it, for now. Better to choose your battles and win the war. He nods his head once, a quick thrust of his chin upwardly, respectfully, then turns his attention to the radio. Song's over, though this one's really fucking great too. The VKTMS' 'Roma Rocket'. DJ must be playing a bunch of stuff to promote the show next week.

The light changes and Gabe chugs them slowly forward. The van needs an oil change badly. Henry makes a note to himself. It's something he can do. He was in the motor pool for two out of his four years over there, working on light wheels. He had a chance to work heavy wheels and track vehicles, but he had it so cushy at HQ, cleaning up jeeps and other light vehicles, that he stayed put. Prior to that, he'd done the whole grunt bit, out in the field, putting in his time, serving watch in the freezing cold and all that. When the opportunity came up to stay warm in the garage and sleep in his own bunk every night, he jumped at it. Sometimes he felt a little guilty about leaving his unit, but it wasn't like there was a war on at the time. Vietnam was over before he went in, and the army was standing down, trying to figure out how the hell to show a good public face again after all that BS over there.

Henry felt pretty lucky about it all. He got in four solid years off the streets, away from his alkie mom and absent dad, biding his time until he could suss out what he was supposed to be doing. He almost ended up staying in and making a career out of the military. He'd won a rack of medals for expert infantryman, army commendation, overseas service, and military proficiency. Still, there was something about the guitar that nagged at him, roping him in during his dreams and waking hours alike. He needed to play the damn thing, and he couldn't do that if he stayed in the army.

Besides, there was something amazing happening to music at the time. Someone turned him onto some underground radio stations in Germany. Henry had started listening to The Sex Pistols, The Clash, Siouxsie & the Banshees, Gen X, Patti Smith, The Undead, and the Ramones. His fingers itched to hold something besides a wrench. He could feel the thrum of a set of Ernie Ball eleven gauge strings on his beat-up Fender Strat back home. Now here he was back here, ripping it up in a band in SF, doing just that. Life really couldn't get much better, no sir.

Well, if San Francisco would clean itself up some. One thing Henry'd brought home from Germany was how amazingly neat and clean her cities were. There were pockets, sure, every city had 'em. But that was mostly where the ragheads and orientals crammed together, lousy proof of immigration laws gone bad. Where the cities had been cleaned up, rid of their 'pest problem' back in the Thirties and Forties, Henry could relax and enjoy himself. He'd come to respect where Germany's leadership had been going back then. Off-base, there was a punk rock club where he'd met up with a small group of neo-Nazis- or National Socialists, as they called themselves- and learned even more that he could respect.

How it was a Jew/Nigger conspiracy to keep families like his down. Henry's dad had left only cause he'd been too weak to stand up to all the Mexicans and Jews moving into their neighborhood, taking over jobs, running decent white Americans out of work and out of their homes. Henry's mom hadn't been much of a drinker before his dad moved out on them, after he'd lost his job at the Port of Oakland to some equal rights hiring bullshit, and found himself a new, clean white life living someplace else. Henry's mom had quickly sunk into rabid alcoholism and basically given up on life. Given up on Henry and anything to do with Henry's dad. In Germany, Henry learned he could blame that on someone besides himself.

His off-base pals had shown him numerously cited facts on the great Jewish supremacist conspiracy, how they'd infiltrated every country's government, legal, and educational systems, taken over multi-national banks, and even run subliminal messages through movies and Jew and Nigger-controlled music. He held firmly to the slogan 'Blood and Honor', deciding he could help in his own small way by bringing clean-minded, blood-pure thinking back home to the States. He wrote about it in his songs, and he staked his arguments against anyone who could stand to benefit from the truth.

Henry did what he could do, keeping to the pure, straight line of racial defense and moral cleanliness that he walked. And he showed others the right way, whenever he could. If only The City would clean itself up some, he could relax a little.

2

He points through the star-cracked windshield to a rumpled-looking business suit opening a late-model cop car door. "Over there. That dude's leaving."

Gabe leans forward for a better look. "Yeah ok..." He punches the gas, then turns towards the line of parked cars and slows down. Max rocks back and forth on the milk crate and holds onto his bass drum again to keep it from rolling off. Henry coughs into his fist. "Um, use your turn signal, Dude."

Gabe shoots his right arm into the air in a Nazi salute. He doesn't really take to all of Henry's anti-semitic, anti-black, anti-this that and the other beliefs. The one thing he likes about being a skin is the clean look, the music, the life. Just not the protocols. "Jahwohl, mein ass-ache." He peeks at Henry from underneath his raised arm. "Rules, man. Only one driver at a time." He focuses on pulling in close to the cars alongside them without clipping anyone, flips the blinker on, and jerks to a stop.

First tour The Shits had gone on late last year, they ended up cobbling together a patchwork rulebook in order to keep from going at each other while on the road. There's a well-thumbed greasy college-lined notebook in the glovebox with all the rules written out as they came up. One of the first was 'Only One Driver At A Time', to avoid too many voices confusing whoever was behind the wheel. Some of the other rules that followed were pretty necessary too: 'Each Band Member Drives Two Hour Shifts' to avoid road fatigue and killing everyone. Henry brought that one out from patrol time in the army. 'Every Night Rotates Straight Edge Driver', so that not one of them gets stuck driving a bunch of drunk assholes too many nights on tour. Evens out the drunk asshole contingency so they all get time in and out of that role, and there's always at least one sober guy at the wheel.

Other rules got tagged on throughout the course of the tour to avoid weird situations: 'No Jerking Off in The Back Seat', 'Stay With The Gear' (after Flipper's van got broken into and all their gear stolen while on tour), 'Don't Mouth Off The Fuzz' so no-one gets themselves hauled off to jail, thereby ending the tour prematurely. Might not be too punk of them, but it gets them to the gig on time and home again in the right number of pieces.

The rumpled suit seems to be having a hard time maneuvering around the van, so Henry jumps out to help with hand signals. The guy behind the wheel visibly flinches and looks scared once he sees Henry's tattoo-covered arms and shaved head. Henry smiles and flexes a little bit. No harm letting this fun go to waste. He holds up both hands though, and waves the driver around the van, bowing his head slightly, snapping his hands just so. Your escort, sir. The driver edges out and guns into oncoming traffic, tires squealing in his getaway. He'll have some kind of a story to tell the kids tonight. How I got away from those scary skinheads.

Henry walks backward into the spot, preventing anyone else from stealing it, using his hand signals to guide Gabe on in. Gabe turns the wheel hard, causing something to squeak painfully from underneath the van, and rolls into the spot, first try. He grins and looks back at Max, who is half-standing already and gathering his gear. Max mutters, "Dude... I am not sitting in back every fucking time we drive through The City." Gabe points a cocked finger at Henry, standing outside the closed door of the Tool and Die. "Talk to the Sarge, señor." Max grimaces. "Yeah... fuck. I'll just skate out to The Deaf Club on my ride this weekend, meet you guys there." They're playing at The Deaf Club, a venue not too far from The Tool and Die, this upcoming Friday. Max turns to the back door. "Let me out, will ya?"

Gabe makes sure everything is locked down, in park, brake on, lights off, before opening his door. He's a good boy scout, and the rest of the band make fun of him for his annoying attention to detail. He climbs out of the van, shuts the driver's door- not too hard- and walks around to the back of the vehicle. He pulls open both back doors and stands back, allowing Max room to start loading out his oversized seedy drum cases.

Henry props the door to the club open- Larry must have answered Henry's rat-a-tat-tat knocking finally- and marches around to the back of the van to start grabbing gear. They load in through the single glass-paned front door, piling their gear just inside the club, before locking up the van and moving the gear downstairs to rehearse.

The place smells of sweat, stale beer and vomit. Gabe doesn't really mind. He loves this scent of real life, and the crackle of a live music venue, even if it is a dump. Henry wrinkles his nose until they get to the cooler, mildewed air of the basement. Too much like ma's vodka-soaked days on the couch, puke-stained hairdresser smocks piled by the back door. She'd wear those smocks so if she vomited on herself, and she often did these days, she could quickly change and keep on drinking.

Max throws himself into their clipped pace now, setting up his drums bit by bit before he shuffles back upstairs for the next load. He's dumped open his hardware bag and is rifling through it for the right stands and odd parts. He's ready for a couple of lines. Maybe he'll see if Amy wants to go for a night skate down through the park later on, skip the show tonight. He tightens the screw on his snare stand and sets it in place by the bass drum.

Fuck this. He gets up and placing both hands on his hips, looks around. The Tool and Die basement is covered in graffiti, layers and layers of it, and shreds of posters hanging off the walls. He reaches up and touches the ceiling, cool beneath his fingertips. Black and red spray-painted pipes run along the length of the room, front to back, making the place look like a steamy old submarine. What's that movie he saw at the art cinema with Gabe and Shelly? Something to do with submarines, anyway. Max thought that was cool. Living underneath all those serious waves, kinda like surfing from inside an enclosed board. Whatever it was, it was rad. Max steps around his drums. Empty half-rack beer boxes litter the floor. He kicks a stray beer bottle and watches as it skitters against the wall behind his kit.

Max bends down, opens his cymbal bag and pulls out his favorite ride. He sets it in place, nestled on its tiny perch of felt, and stands back.

"I'll be right back, Dudes."

Before they can say anything, he gallops up the narrow

walled-in stairwell to the roomier gallery space upstairs. At first, he squints in the bright fluorescents arrayed as some sort of artsy display near the basement entryway, then strides over to the back door, which is slightly ajar.

"Larry? H'lo! You here?" Max peeks around the doorway, one hand reaching into his back pocket for his wallet. Larry rustles in from the bathroom in back, behind the tiny kitchenette just inside the small, enclosed room.

"Hey there Max. What's going on?"

He'd just done his hair, bleached reddish-blond at the tips, and is pre-occupied with what to wear tonight. He knows what Max wants though, and since Max is such a hunk, and a sweetie besides, Larry's willing to take a break from his routine.

Larry leans against the partition between the kitchenette and the rest of his living space. He'd built it onto the back of the main gallery here as an office, and added the bathroom and kitchenette as a sort of afterthought once he realized he could actually live here too. He never sleeps much anyway, so the late shows don't bother him at all.

He licks his lips and bats his eyelashes, just once. Max knows Larry likes him. For a straight boy, he's not dumb.

He's not a people-user either, which marks up points in his favor. He just knows Larry's interested and doesn't need it spelled out. And he doesn't make an issue out of it. They both like speed, and Larry likes Max. So why not do a few lines together every now and then? As in every week when The Shits come to rehearse? There's no harm in flirting, and in getting high while doing so. That way everyone has a good time.

Max smiles shyly. He's still not very good at being flirted with. He's more used to the cool-cheeked stand-offish method that Amy has. Still, he doesn't mind being ogled a little. He knows he's in great shape from surfing and playing the drums. So he's okay with Larry coming onto him from a distance. If you can't find admiration where you want it, why not take it where you can get it? And besides, the speed is always great, though today, he brought something along.

"So... wanna do a few lines? I'm almost all set up. Gotta wait for Henry to change his strings out." He opens his wallet. "I've got something here..." He plucks a small rolled-up cellophane packet from behind the two damp dollars in his billfold and holds it out for Larry to inspect. Larry waves his hands no.

"No no. I've got some great stuff from my new source.

You have *got* to try it out." He pushes off from the wall and steps into the small room to his left. "Let me set it up."

Max puts his stash away then, something to share with Amy later on. He waits for Larry to arrange the gold-marbled mirror tile with its chipped edges on the messy heavy oak coffee table that takes up a good portion of the room. Larry sits on the partly deflated inflatable red plastic couch, pushes a stack of magazines onto the floor, and taps a good portion of speed out onto the mirror.

"Get yourself a drink," he offers as he chops at the sparkly white crystals. His eyes remain intent on the growing pile of white powder, so Max looks around for a bottle. "Whatchya got? Oh, never mind. I see." He sees the half-drunk bottle of rum on the kitchen counter, nearly hidden by the pile of dirty glasses and coffee cups. "Nah... I'm cool. Thanks though. I'm not much of a rum drinker."

Larry holds a short-cut straw up to Max. "Here ya go." Max takes the straw and kneels down next to the table, opposite Larry. "Thanks." He looks up at Larry and smiles. This is always a good time. Even if Henry does have issues with Larry being gay, he's all right in Max's book. Larry smiles coyly. "Oh never you mind. Enjoy kiddo. It's my pleasure. You know..."

Max turns his head and barks out a quick laugh away from the carefully laid out lines. He turns back to the mirror, and mumbles, smiling, "Cut it out, Dude. I almost spewed this shit all over the place!" He lowers his head, remembering when he had to hold back his long blond hair to do this in another lifetime. That's another advantage to shaving his head.

Max snorts up one line, then another, alternating nostrils. Oh... he loves that plastic taste, that chemical burn... The lights behind his eyelids immediately brighten. He can feel his brain turning on, lighting up.

"Oh man. This is gonna be good, I can tell." He hands the straw over to Larry, who makes sure to avoid touching Max's hand when taking it. Don't want to make the boy nervous now. He sniffs through both nostrils quickly to make sure his nose is clear, then leans over and partakes. Oh this is nice. Too bad ol' Maxy here doesn't want to hang out and have some *more* fun. Larry closes his eyes as the speed makes its way to the back of his skull. He's looking forward to the show. There's always some boy-toy willing to indulge.

Max stands up. "Thanks Larry. I gotta get downstairs before Sarge has a fit. You going to the show in Berkeley next week?"

Larry sniffles a little and placing the pad of one thumb against each nostril in turn, snorts harder to ensure he isn't losing any of his high. He leans back onto the couch, making it squeak and fart beneath his shifting weight. "Oh yeah. I was thinking I'd make my way out there early, hit some dumpsters. You know they're playing here tonight too, right?" Max nods. "Well, so I figured I'd hit the Embarcadero, then see what's new and shakin' out by the train tracks over there. Last time I went out there, I found a box full of transistors. Remember that sculpture I did?"

Max nods again. Oh this stuff is good. He's tapping his fingers against the wall in anticipation of getting back downstairs. "Yeah, I think so. You were doing those melted 45's then too, weren't you?" Larry had gone through an ashtray period, when he'd half-baked stacks of 45's into curly oyster shell-shaped bowls. He gave them away with the entrance fee to shows for a week or so, until too many of them ended up shattered in shiny piles of odd-shaped shards downstairs. He wore them as hats for a while after that, then moved on to something new.

Larry smiles fondly. "Oh I'm so glad you remember those! Ok, get yourself downstairs. I have to keep getting ready."

Max turns to leave just as Henry bellows up the stairs, "Max! Quit fucking around! Let's GO!" Max rolls his eyes, here they go. "Jahwohl! See ya Lare." He trots over to the stairwell and pauses suddenly. There, rolled up into a tight burrito against the wall, is a wad of cash. He bends down and scoops it up. Sure enough, it's bills. Maybe twenty, thirty bucks? He shoves it into his pocket, figuring he'll have time later to count it out, then takes the stairs two at a time, using the walls to slow his descent down a skosh.

3

He leaps into the basement room, appreciating how cool and almost frosty it feels down here after the somewhat stifling closeness of Larry's well-lit apartment upstairs. "Ok, Dudes. I'm almost set up. You ready?" Max kicks open his hardware bag and grabs the throne stand.

Gabe is busy concentrating on tuning his bass, leaning against the support pole in the middle of the room. He hasn't been playing all that long and is still unsure exactly how to tune up. But he manages to get something close to the right sound, at least, what sounds right to his untrained ear. Henry had come back from Germany pushing to get a band going, so Gabe and Max bought corresponding instruments, and they started up The Shits. Max had played drums in high school, and Henry has played guitar ever since anyone can remember, so Gabe is the only one of the three who's new to this whole music thing.

His folks paid for bass lessons in the beginning, and Shelly bought him a stack of how-to books. She used to come to their gigs until she got too caught up in the heavy dealing she's been up to lately. So Gabe tapes their shows every once in a while and drops off copies when he visits her pad. Of course, last time he ended up in the hospital, so he's not too sure about seeing his sister these days. At least, not at her 'office'. He's been trying to get her to come meet him someplace for lunch the past few weeks. But she's been seeing this Middle Eastern guy lately- Gabe thinks it's her H source- and he doesn't really like it at all. Not that it's about the whole Nazi bullshit that Henry espouses. Just 'cause the guy's dark skinned or a raghead or whatever, Gabe's cool with that. There's just something about him that's creepy. Gabe met him once and didn't care for the way he seemed so possessive of Shelly. Like her brother can't even get close? That's bothering him even more than what to do about Carla. Gabe feels like he's got some seriously loose ends, and he's not sure which one to tie up first.

Henry is standing over his pedal board, clicking something on and off again with the heavy tip of his right steel-toed boot. He knows he shouldn't play in his boots- he keeps cracking the switches on his pedals- but he just can't bring himself to step onstage, or in public for that matter, in Vans. Besides, these are his all-time favorite boots. He picked them up at a sidewalk sale about six months ago. Some fag had a bunch of Yugoslavian military boots and backpacks arranged all nice and pretty out in front of his rainbow-colored Haight apartment. He had some story about traveling with a choir group over there and buying up all these boots and rucksacks as a favor to someone he met. Supposedly they're not doing so well over there. Henry figures it's the whole Jew situation, though this guy wasn't worth wasting his breath on educating properly. Henry politely listened as long as he could to the guy's wincey stories, then ended up buying a pair of boots for himself and a pair two sizes too large for Amy, back when they were still seeing each other. She still wears the boots, though he remembers, they give her blisters.

He flashes briefly on an image of Amy leaning against the back outer wall at the Mab, wearing a tiny leopard print t-shirt, some kind of shiny stretchy tight pants, and those boots. She looked amazingly hot. Better not let Sophie know he still thinks about Amy that way. Fuck it, he doesn't really. It's just that get up, those boots, her sorta cowgirl lope and the way she carries herself.

Sophie, on the other hand, is *all tough mama*. She's stacked and can wrastle around with Henry the way he likes it. That is one super fucking incredibly hot chick, *and* racially appropriate, of course. Henry realizes he's distracted by thoughts of Sophie, and before pushing on, thinks to himself, that's good. She'll do.

He sighs. Ok, back to reality. Fuck it. He'll have to re-solder this fucking Big Muff pedal again. Make a list. The van, the pedal... what's next?

Max starts playing through a litany of drum rolls, kicks, paradiddles and flams. Gabe is still tuning up, but he's close. At least he doesn't sound too out of tune. A little flat maybe, as always, but Henry will tune down too. Easier and faster than coaching Gabe to tune properly. This actually gets The Shits their unique sound. They play a little flat, and a lot too loud, which ends up making them sound distorted as all fuck, and really great. Sort of like a funeral dirge, turned up to high speed.

Henry slams a chord, hard, and chokes it off. "Hey!!" He barks. "Let's just run through both sets, straight through. If you fuck up, keep going, like it's a show." He holds up his worn Strat in query.

"Yeah ok. Sounds good." Max answers, wiping at the back of his neck with one hand. Gabe notices that Max is sweating and a little wild eyed. Little fucker. he went upstairs and got high again with Larry. He's gonna have to learn to share that shit. Man, Gabe shakes his head, admonishing himself. He *never* thinks harsh thoughts like that! He is definitely stressed about this whole thing with Shelly and that Ahab dude. Well, and Carla. Something's definitely got to give. Gabe looks up and around. The other two make eye contact with him. Yup, they're ready.

"One Two Three Four! One Two Three!" Max sings out.

"Whatchya gonna do with that evil eye?
Whatchya gonna think when I kiss it goodbye?
Whatchya gonna be in your afterlife?
Fuckin' Dead! That's What! Fuckin' DEAD!"

Henry has a smooth voice, which he disguises by shouting, loud and hoarse, as harshly as he can. The other two sing along in unison on the second half of each line, harmonizing as best they can with Henry, doubling up on the backing vocals. The whole effect is like that of a couple of badly tuned lawn mowers, somehow playing sonically and in harmony side by side. Everyone eats it up.

Their first single, recorded right before they went on their first tour and self-released, sold out 500 copies. They'd sat around Henry's room with stacks of boxes all around them, hand-folding paper jackets, pressing labels onto both sides of each 45 by hand, addressing bubble-wrap envelopes with heavy black crayons and sharpies, mailed one by one, for the most part, to addresses on the stapled list Henry'd acquired from East Bay Ray of the Dead Kennedys. About 100 sold at the Fire Station, the local punk 'mall' on 16th. The rest they sent to radio stations across the States and sold through word of mouth. They'd received letters addressed to Pat's place, asking for copies, folded dollar bills pressed between sweaty sheets of paper, for months.

On the road, they had to sell shitty tapes with hand-drawn labels Shelly paid to have copied off. The tapes flew off the table at every show, and The Shits are getting seriously stable airplay all over the country now on every major city underground punk rock radio show. They even have an interview coming up with Flipside supposedly next week. At least, that's what some chick said over the phone to Henry the other day. They're all supposed to show up at The Tool and Die for the interview and photos on Tuesday at two.

Funny thing is that Henry can really sing like an angel. Sometimes when no one is paying attention, least of all Henry, he sings along to whatever tune is in his head or on the radio, sounding smooth as lubricant, all choirboy. Gabe and Max give each other 'that' look, the one that says 'don't say a fucking word.'

But when he sings in The Shits, he growls and bellows, forcing his voice into this megaphone-like sand-scratched gravel. That, paired with the two others' slightly flat synchronized harmonies and the hard bright crash of surf-like drums, sonically tainted flat bass and severely distorted guitar, equals gold to punk audiences everywhere. The Shits are on to something here.

They run through their first set with only a couple of clams.

Henry messes up, forgetting the changes on 'Hell Hound' they'd added a few weeks back, and coming in too late on 'Mama Did It' when he wasn't paying attention to the set list.

Max is covered in a sheen of sweat, oozing out of his pores, trickling down his back, the crack of his ass... he can even feel sweat between his toes. His brain is on fire though. This shit is GREAT. He feels bad about the stuff getting wet maybe in his wallet. Can't stop now though. He and Amy will have to shoot it up. Hey... there's something titillating about her shooting up his sweat. He wonders if he should tell her.

Suddenly Henry stops playing. Max continues to play the hardcore train beat he's got going, but Henry doesn't cut back in. Gabe stops too, his last off-key note ringing out. Max stops with a crash on his high hat. He looks over at Henry.

"What the fuck, Dude? I thought we weren't supposed to stop?"

Henry sinks down into a crouch. He's holding his guitar in a strange way. Max can't really see it all that well, but... is his mind playing tricks on him now or is Henry's guitar at a funny angle? He half stands from his drum throne to see over the bass drum.

"Hey Sarge? What the hell is going on?"

Henry whimpers a little. That is not a sound an ex-military man should make. Max stands up entirely and leans over his drum kit. What the fuck? Henry is cradling the body of his guitar against his stomach while holding the neck at a complete right angle in his left hand. Strings still connect the two halves of the guitar, but the neck is definitely not attached to the Strat any longer.

Henry speaks up. "Uh guys... I can't fucking believe this. But um... my guitar just broke."

Gabe nearly drops his bass. "No fucking way..." He fumbles with the strap, then pulls it over his head and leans the bass up against his amp. It feeds back a scratchy little ghost of some Mexican radio station, and Gabe switches the amp off. He steps quickly around the center pole to where Henry is crouched, rocking, crooning to his guitar. Max makes his way around the drums and stands over Henry, opposite Gabe. They both look down in disbelief. Looks like the guitar neck just snapped off, and not cleanly. A thin jagged fan of blond maple feathers out from where it is still attached, below the break, to the guitar body at the Strat's neck joint. Gabe notices the last five frets still somewhat in place, two of them hanging off jaggedly like something took a crunchy bite off the neck of the guitar.

Henry is holding the headstock up against his cheek. Gabe kneels down to get a closer look. This is bad. Henry hasn't worked since he got fired from the news stand downtown. He was caught stealing gum, though he swears the Korean owners were just looking for an excuse to get rid of him, distrusting his tattoos and Nazi epithets. He'd interviewed for the job in long sleeves and his watchman's cap, then surprised his new bosses by showing up for work in Hitler-sloganed t-shirts with cut-off sleeves and his thickly studded leather belt and wristbands. It had taken some time, but they eventually went at him one afternoon as he was popping a piece of gum into his mouth. He'd paid for it, but they claimed he hadn't and fired him on the spot.

Since then, he's hit up the Haight food bank, and lived off of whatever Sophie, Amy and Val bring by Pat's for food and libations. He gets free beer at shows and spends a lot of time writing and doing band-related work, so all in all, it hasn't been that bad. But he definitely doesn't have the money to fix this. And this Strat has been his baby for years, before he went into the army, definitely longer than any relationship he's ever had with someone on two legs. It had been his uncle's guitar before he gave it to Henry his first year of junior high school. It got him through his dad's exodus and kept him company while his mom dove into the bottle over time. Henry presses one side of his mouth to the neck, a small string of spittle connecting his lips to the sweat-shined wood.

Max shoves both hands into the front pockets of his jeans. The fingers of his right hand brush up against the burrito-wad of cash he'd found earlier upstairs. He rocks back onto his heels and pulls the cash out. Keeping his eyes locked on Henry holding onto the broken pieces of his guitar, Max folds the bills out flat. "Hey, Dudes…" He glances down and starts sorting the money into ones, fives, hey! There's a ten, and a fifty! "Dudes." Gabe looks at Max's hands.

"What the fuck…? Where'd you get that?" He turns his head slightly to the side. "Man, you ain't running tricks with ol' Lare upstairs, now, are ya?" He laughs, but only half-jokingly. Seriously, where'd Max get that sort of money?

Max shakes his whole body, like a dog shedding water. Shake it off. "No way, man. Don't even. No, I found this upstairs, by the top of the stairs. Right by the door. It's…" He keeps sorting bills. "… a lot of money, it looks like. Gimme a second. Let me count it out." Henry looks up, face still pressed to the light blond maple neck of his broken Strat.

Max finishes sorting the bills and starts counting. By the time he reaches two hundred, he pauses. "Hey Henry. Dude, this is really fucking weird. But I think I was supposed to find this and give it to you. Here." He hands the pile of money down to Henry. Henry takes a deep breath, looking down at his beloved guitar. Then back up to Max's hand hovering before him, the money so close he can smell it. He stands up and presses the guitar body against his belly, holding it in place with his left arm. Gripping the neck tightly in his left hand, he reaches for the money with his right.

"Seriously. This is too fucking cool. Thanks, man." Henry takes the proffered cash and looks into Max's eyes. Max nods in encouragement and places one hand lightly on his high hat. Man, if his drum kit busted up like that, he'd be a mess. And he hasn't had it for all that long. This is intense. Henry turns his eyes to the floor and wipes at them with his right hand, the wad of cash brushing up against his forehead.

Gabe and Max make eye contact. The man is crying a little. There's no way this gets out of this room. No fucking way.

"Hey man, it's cool." Gabe wants to reach out and touch Henry's arm, but he knows the gesture would be taken all wrong. He looks down at the cheap plastic watch on his wrist. "Look, it's only 4:30. Let's head over to that dude up on Haight's house. What's his name? Blower something? He fixes shit like this. I know he can do something, or at least he'll know what to do, where to go." He raises his hands in query, and his whole face lights up in that 'whaddaya say?' look. *This* is something he can fix, right here and right now. "Come on guys. Let's pack it up and get over there."

Henry holds the guitar out, away from his body. He's not quite sure *how* to pack it up. Ok, place it back in the case and be careful with it. "Yeah, ok. Let's do it. Thanks guys. Really, that's above and beyond..." He moves over to his case and kicks it open with one steel-toed boot. He reverently lays the guitar out in its' red furred bed lining and touches the break gently with the fingers of his left hand. Henry closes the case and latches it shut, reaches over to flip his amp off, and shoves his strap into the limp olive gig bag at his feet. The cash goes into the crisp right front pocket of his jeans. He turns to Gabe and Max.

"Cool. Yeah, let's do this."

Gabe lugs amps and gig bags upstairs while Henry helps Max break down his drum kit. Something about the broken guitar has calmed Max down. He's still high, grinding his teeth a little, but no longer sweating or antsy. He quickly loads up his gear and he and Henry cart it upstairs. Henry leaves his guitar case for last, then gently lifts it in both hands and carries it up the narrow stairway to the open gallery.

Max has started loading out, and Gabe is standing watch at

the door, honoring rule #4 'Stay With The Gear'. Max plays Van Rubik's Cube, packing everything in just so, on the dregs of his high. He grabs the last of his gear, his cymbal bag and tom case, and pauses at the door.

"Ok Dudes. That's it. You got your guitar, let's head."

Gabe looks at Max. "Man, you mind sitting in back...?"

Max shakes his head no. Hell no, this is extenuating circumstances if he ever heard of any. "Fuck, no worries. Get in the van."

Henry smiles then and looks at the other two before stepping into the hazy San Francisco late afternoon street. "Damn right man. Get in the fuckin' van." It's what he'd said to get The Shits on the road the first time they went out. It's what'll get him back on his feet again, no matter what happens to Blondie, his guitar, here.

Larry steps out from the back room as the front door snaps closed. "They didn't even say goodbye..." he muses to himself. "Was it something I said?"

"San Francisco is a mad city – inhabited for the most part by perfectly mad people."— **Rudyard Kipling**
Don't Fuck With Blondie

1

Babs rolls over, trying to get comfortable on the lumpy, cardboard-thin mattress. Her heart is beating too fast and too loud though, and she can't relax. She knows it was that last line she did right before turning off the kitchen light. But still, she'd thought it would calm her down enough to get *some* sleep. She sighs and rolls over again onto her back.

Maybe if she tries tightening her muscles and then relaxing them. She remembers that from some camp she went to years ago. Her mom and dad had sent her, worried about her new friends, the fact that she'd bleached her hair and didn't seem interested in food anymore. She'd had fun at the camp, participating in the daily group sessions, private one on ones, and various activities designed to break the kids out of their shells. She liked that her parents were interested enough to send her there. And she liked acting so serious, like she was so deeply connected with her feelings.

She fooled them though. She played their games and showed up on time, shared her feelings, and cried on cue.

But there was no fucking way she would ever really let anyone in. It was so much safer to put on an act and hide way deep down inside. At the end of the week-long session, the therapists told her parents they didn't think she was ready to let go of whatever she was hanging on to. She'd shrugged and looked out the window, through the hazy screened-in mosquito netting, and made up a little ditty inside her head, 'damned tootin', doo-de-doop-de-doo'.

The ride home had been deliberately silent. Her parents wouldn't even let her listen to her Walkman. She glanced down at it every so often longingly, laying on the seat next to her, but she held out. As soon as they'd arrived home, she stomped through the house to her room off the garage, slammed the door, and cranked Adam and the Ants' 'Stand and Deliver' as loud as her little boombox could handle, over and over again, poising her finger over the rewind button until the song finished each time, ready to start it up again.

Now, where was she? Oh right, tighten your leg muscles, then relax. Tighten your shoulders, then relax. Oo, this wasn't going to work. Babs could feel her muscles tightening in response to her mind's command, but there was no letting go. They just stayed tensed up. Fuck this. She sits up and turns to lean against the wall.

Babs sits cross-legged and forces the small of her back into the wall. She takes a deep breath and lets it out quickly, resigned to staying up longer. Well, maybe there's something she can do? What time is it, anyway?

Problem is, she doesn't feel safe leaving the confines of her room, this little odd-shaped maid's quarters off the back of the kitchen. Babs has been staying with Annie for three weeks now, cleaning and doing odd jobs for her. But Annie has laid down the law. In no way should Babs consider herself an actual roommate. This is Annie's squat, and Babs has no say in it.

Babs has made do, stacking her collection of albums in their sagging, busted peach crates along one wall, pushing her thin, old twin mattress against another, and taping her favorite postcards and posters to the walls around the room. She likes the room. It has the only fireplace in the apartment, inside which Babs has placed her altar. She lights candles and incense, and does her best to pay homage to the black arts. Babs isn't in a coven, but she likes to think of herself as a witch anyway. She tries to cast spells on people every now and then and finds comfort in the litany of mumbled ritual prayers over her fetishes, candles and small bottles of various tinctures carefully laid out inside the fireplace.

Ok then, Babs figures she'll work on the new spell she's been reciting every day for the past week. She uncrosses her legs and carefully tiptoes her way across the room to the light switch by the door. She doesn't want to step on her pet rat like she nearly did a few days ago.

She loves the *idea* of the rat, Luna, with its' pink-rimmed eyes and crinkly little nose, though she doesn't love it, like she could a cat or dog. Still, walking around town with the rat on her shoulder, Babs feels cool and different, perfectly punk enough to shock anyone not in tune with her lifestyle and the way she presents herself. She wraps Luna around her neck as they bounce down to Petrini's or the corner store, Luna's long pink tail unfurling down Babs' shirt. She constantly has to capture Luna as the rat scampers down her arm or coat front, replacing it time after time on her shoulder, nestled against her neck. Stroking Lunas' soft white fur calms Babs down. She sits in her room and runs one hand over Luna's pelt, feeding her bits of celery and carrot with the other. Luna sits up on Babs' lap, her tiny sharp claws digging into Babs' thin flesh. She sings to Luna and tells her what she's thinking. Babs feels like Luna understands her. Maybe the rat is her familiar, after all.

Right now though, Babs has no idea where Luna has gone off to. Usually she finds her curled up in a nest on Babs messy, unmade bed, or tearing shreds out of the piles of photos Babs keeps stacked around her room. Earlier tonight, when she'd come home from panhandling up and down Haight, Babs had carefully opened the door and found no sign of the small white creature. Babs had searched and called out Luna's name, but the rat stayed out of sight.

Babs sighs again and leans forward at the waist, reaching for her toes, feeling that delicious pull on her hamstrings. Wrapping the first finger of each hand around each big toe, Babs pulls herself forward, down, deeper into the stretch. The pain in her legs eases up and shifts instead to a delicious sensation of her muscles pulling, stretching, tightening and releasing at once.

She lets go, and standing up, laces her fingers together and turns her palms up to the ceiling. She stretches her arms high over her head and pushes her shoulders back slightly in their sockets so she can feel her shoulder blades nearly touch like folded wings.

"Ahhhh..." Sometimes, Babs wishes she'd never quit gymnastics. She loved to tumble on the mats, run and jump off the horse, and swing from the uneven parallel bars. But she could never apply herself to any of it with 100% dedication like some of the other girls did. She liked winning but couldn't be bothered to do all the work to get there. After repeatedly failing to qualify for competitions on the local county team, she quit. Babs wonders if she'd tried just a little harder, if she would have ever been good enough to go farther. That was a long time ago; guess she'll never know.

The sound of heavy boots clomping up the front stairs brings Babs back into the room, out of her thoughts. The front door opens, and Annie's rich, rough voice fills the squat.

"Hah! Whataya mean you had no idea?! Don't you guys, like, know *everything* about each other? I mean, don't you share, like, secrets and stuff when you're on the road?"

Babs wonders who Annie has brought back to the squat with her. She lays on her back and presses down into the sheets, as though to listen more quietly. She hears a man's voice– a *man's* voice!– from the front room, as Annie and her guest move from the entryway into the front living area, with its turreted windows and leaded glass cabinets that separate that room from Annie's boudoir.

Annie laughs flirtatiously, a long, loud spurt of laughter that starts as a near-cackle and trails off into a tinkly, oddly feminine trill. Her guest must have said something amusing, or she wants him to think she thinks so. His voice comes murmuring through the thin walls, indistinct, unclear. Babs wishes she could hear what he's saying, figure out who he is.

Then, "Aaaahh. What a cool pad. You live here alone?" His voice doesn't tell her who he is, but Babs guesses he's not a regular guest by the question itself. Funny, who around The City doesn't know Annie? Hmm. Need more information.

"Oh yeah. I couldn't stand to have someone else living here. I need all the space, for you know, what*ever* comes up. Hmm. Like *this*?" Annie giggles again, though to Babs it sounds a bit evil and menacing. She hears movement in Annie's room, separated from Babs' little maid quarters by the wall and fireplace between them. The sound carries through quite well. Babs can hear the rustling of cloth, and what sounds like an artillery of belts hitting the pocked wood floor. More mumbling, though it may very well be moans, meant to impart encouragement. From what Babs can remember anyway, that's how it goes. It's been so long since she's let anyone touch her that way.

Either way, huh. Annie's getting it on with some *guy*?! As far as Babs knows, Annie is all woman for all women, period. Oh well, surprise, surprise. Maybe hell froze over or something. She turns over onto her stomach and lays her chin across her folded arms. Closing her eyes, she continues to eavesdrop. The noises coming from the next room are unmistakably the melody of sex. Sounds like two large animals rutting, bumping again and again into the wall against which Annie's bed is arranged. If Babs had been able to sleep tonight, she'd surely have been awakened by all that ruckus now.

First there's a bang bang bang against the wall, then rustling cloth and murmurs. Then bang bang bang again. It's all a bit tedious, if you ask me, thinks Babs. She rolls her eyes and continues to listen, trying to guess what's happening now.

The racket mounts in volume through the brick and plaster. Someone, Babs figures it must be the guy, starts groaning steadily, "Aah, aah, aah!" Each 'aah' timed with a thrust-bang, bang, bang against the wall. Hey, good rhythm, you could dance to this, Babs smiles to herself.

"Slow down, baby!" Babs hears Annie command. "Woah...!" But the steady "Aah, aah, aah" goes on, louder, more insistent. "Fuck man! Slow DOWN!" Annie bellows out. But the train keeps chugging along. Babs smiles harder.

The "Aah, aah" abruptly strangles to a choked close "Unh, mph!" Babs lifts her head in the silence. Suddenly, something large hits the floor causing the wall between the two rooms to shudder.

"What the FUCK?!" Annie screams out, the fearsome bellow of a bull cow. Babs sits up, alarmed.

"What the FUCK was THAT?! I TOLD you to slow DOWN! You fucking pig. You little fucking pig! Fucking MEN!" Babs hears the rustling of clothing being gathered up, clanking metal, and the light thud of something or someone being shoved around. She stands and grabs a pair of fusty black knickers off the floor. Quickly pulling them on, she quietly opens the door onto the kitchen so she can maybe get a peek at what's unfolding in the other room.

Annie's guest, no longer welcome, is being bullied and pushed towards the front door. His slight, dark figure is dwarfed by Annie's 200 plus pound bulk. As he shies away from her blows and kicks, he tries to pull his pants up, all while dropping and scooping up a collection of studded leather belts, boots, and his heavy leather jacket.

Annie continues to scream at him, belittling his puny manhood and his sorry excuse for sex, if that's what he calls sex. She is inspired with her expletives and abuse. Babs listens cheerfully, only slightly alarmed at what Annie might do next. Babs has never seen Annie this cranked up.

Annie reaches behind the potted plant that sits near the front entry alcove. Yup, sure enough, when her hand emerges from behind the leafy fronds of the plant, it holds Annie's prized twenty-two ounce ash slugger, a baseball bat so scarred from bashing parked cars and streetlight poles, it's taken on the loving name DiMaggio, in nod to Annie's one obsession.

She picks up the bat with both hands wrapped tightly around the base, and raising it above her head, Annie begins to swing.

"You little FUCKER! Actually, you're a no-GOOD fucker! Man, you can't even WAIT to get me off! FUCK you and the little FUCKing tour bus you rode in on!"

Babs steps around the corner of the doorway into the kitchen, trying to get a better look at Annie's hapless guest. She sees a slight cowering form trying to defend itself from the onslaught of DiMaggio. She can just make out a canopy of half scraggly-half sculpted shoulder-length bleached hair. Some rocker guy, by the looks of his hair and clothing. But who?

The rocker manages to pull the door open, and pants held up with one hand, throws his belongings down the stairwell. Stumbling, he takes the stairs two at a time after them. Annie is in hot pursuit, and she's growing scarier by the second. Now she's huffing like the big bad wolf as she chases him down the stairs.

"Phuh, phuh, phuh!" She swings the bat around and around, smashing holes into the walls of the stairwell as she descends swiftly behind her prey. "I'm gonna GET you, you no good little FUCKer! Phuh, phuh, phuh!"

Babs creeps through the kitchen and starts for the stairwell, but then, not wanting Annie to see her, heads for the front turreted windows. With her face pressed against the chilled, moist windowpane, she watches the thin figure of the blond rocker stumble down below as he attempts to run while pulling up his pants. Clutching his boots, jacket and belts to his chest, he turns his head wildly this way and that, searching for a way out of this nightmare.

Annie emerges from the doorway, huffing and puffing and wielding the bat over her head, now poised like a samurai, prepared for battle. The rocker begins to pick up speed and run towards the park as Annie follows him. The streetlights cast their dramatic shadows down the sidewalk and street as she advances purposefully, though it looks like she's allowing him to get away.

2

Babs laughs as she strains to see more, "Wow..." She's witnessed a lot of strange things in her time on the streets and away from home, but this was special. She wishes there was someone there with her to attest to what just happened. She turns from the window, and chilled, wraps her arms around her nearly non-existent breasts.

Well, now what? There's no *way* she can fall asleep after all that brouhaha. She decides to wait for Annie's return to see if she can find out what the heck that was all about. Obviously, bad sex, but beyond that- who was the guy in the first place?

Babs crosses the room to the stereo displayed against the dividing wall between the front room and Annie's boudoir. She squints at the stereo face for a second, then pushes the right buttons, lighting everything up. She sorts through the slim stack of albums leaning against the wall, and chooses one of her favorites, Bauhaus's 'Bela Lugosi's Dead'. It's a single, but Babs doesn't mind playing it repeatedly. Speed goes well with repetition.

She slips the EP from its cardboard sleeve and places it on the turntable. Making sure to set the speed to the correct setting, she lifts the needle into place and relaxes at that first soft scritch of needle to vinyl. Ahhhh... here it comes. Babs can listen to this song over and over again. This, and Patti Smith's 'Horses'. Especially when she's shooting up: just as the speed hits her bloodstream and she gets that lovely surge of white light. She loves to time it so that Patti's voice incants 'Horses horses horses' at just the right moment. Even just listening to these songs already high makes everything seem so fresh and alive, always just right.

As the song starts to unspool, Babs thinks how the lyrics are so eerie and wicked... exactly how she envisions her own eerie, wicked self. If she had a theme song, this would be it.

She lies down on the floor and spreads her arms and hands out into an extended cross shape, like that Michelangelo etching she has tacked up on her wall. She closes her eyes and nods lightly to the pulsing rhythm of the song. "... Undead undead undead..." Babs smiles to herself. This. Is. Perfect. Can't sleep, might as well enjoy myself.

Babs attention fades a little. She can still hear the song, driving, knocking into her brain, yet she has pulled back from her body just enough to not quite be all there. She finds herself hovering overhead: she's so pretty, so slight, so pale and helpless. And oh the song... oh this life. Babs is absolutely content in this moment: here, yet not here.

The 7" finishes and the needle softly sweeps towards the spindle, then lifts, and sets back down at the start of the small disk. Sweet Mary! Thinks Babs. It's set to replay all by itself!

She lies there, unmoving, on the floor, breathing in the song, feeling it course through her veins. If only Annie never came home. Then speak of the bottle blonde version of the devil, Annie's thick-soled boots hit the stairs. Mumbling to herself as she stomps heavily upon each riser, Annie uses the bat as a sort of crutch, a third little clomp after every other footfall. Babs sits up and tries to look casual. Oh yeah, I'm just hanging out half naked, sprawled on the floor in NOT-my apartment, at what? Four o'clock in the morning? She arranges an innocent expression on her face and turns her upper torso towards the door.

Annie's enormous frame fills the doorway. "Hey!" She's surprised to find Babs sitting in the middle of the front room, though not so by her choice of music. Annie knows this is one of Babs' favorite songs.

"What are you doing up? Or are you *up*?" She runs the bat smoothly through her free hand and swings it like a golf club before placing the head of the bat flat on the floor and leaning with both hands onto the handle. "No, really. What's up? What are you doing out here?"

Babs is uncertain whether Annie is unhappy with her appearance in the front room, though the front door had been left open, so really, better her 'non-roommate' than anyone else, she supposes. Either way, she feels threatened, as always, by Annie's stance.

"Uh, well, I heard something out here, and by the time I got up and came out, there was no-one here. So I thought... I thought I'd wait to see if you were ok or needed something."

Annie presses her lips together and smiles faintly. "What if I didn't come back?"

"I... don't know. I didn't think of that." Babs shrugs her shoulders in a gesture of 'Don't ask me'. "I just figured I'd wait for you." She creases her brow and turns back towards the stereo, looking down at her lap. "So, where were you? What's going on?"

Annie laughs, her more natural chortle- not that fake giggle she'd put on for whoever the guy was. She picks up the bat and replaces it behind the plant, then turns and sighs, clapping her hands to her wide, rounded hips. "You'll never believe who was here tonight."

Babs crosses her legs and spins around on the floor so

that she is facing Annie, looking up at her, with that innocent look on her face. Hurry up, Annie, she thinks, spill the beans. She leans back onto both hands and notices a faint light coming through the windows. It's later than she thought.

"Ok, yeah, so... who? Someone I know?"

Annie grins, all teeth and menace. "Well, no. Not really. You might have *heard* of him..."

"Ok... who?!" Babs rocks forward, listing towards Annie in anticipation.

Annie looks around, reaches for the faded worn velveteen chair beside her, and plops herself down for her audience. "Ok. So you know how Larry promised me he'd take me to a show for my birthday?" Babs nods yes. "So, he stopped by yesterday on his way round the neighborhood and told me to get all dolled up for a special show, that he'd stop by later to pick me up *in style*." Annie emphasizes 'In style' with a flick of her hands as she kicks off her boots.

"So I curled my hair, did myself all up nice and sexy, and wore that pale blue satin formal Bella traded me for some speed. You know the one I'm talking about? Have you seen it? Slits up to *here*," Annie extends her leg to one side and gestures to her upper thigh, smiling. Babs nods in agreement. She hasn't seen the dress yet, but she can imagine all ten yards of it, ha.

"Yeah, so Larry picked me up in a yellow cab, er-yesterday- and wouldn't tell me where we were going. I kept guessing, but no dice. I had no idea..."

Babs leans in, excited by the story now, "Where did he take you?!"

Annie leans back into her chair and taps a cigarette out of her lamé cigarette case. She places it in the brass cigarette holder and lights up. "Alright already..." She grins at Babs, knowing she has a captive audience for this great tale. Now how to tell it right? She takes a beat, inhaling and blowing out the smoke through teeth clamped around the cool brass mouthpiece. "Ok, so the ride took forever. I mean, down through the Mission, I'm thinking a nice Mexican dinner? Then over to Bayshore Heights, way the fuck out in nowhere. Then I figured it out. We were going to Cow Palace, right?"

Babs nods, and realizes she's grinding her jaw, so she snaps her mouth open and shut to release the tension. "Oh right. Was there a show?"

Annie smiles, "Oh yeah, there was a show. Ratt played with

some band called the Great White Shark, or something like that. I dunno. But Larry– get this– had the cab drop us off at some back entrance area, where we showed our IDs and were let in to this long hallway area. We had to make our way up all these stairs and passageways to... tada!!" Annie waves her hands in the air on each side of her face like confetti fluttering in the air. "Backstage! He had *backstage passes*!" She's grinning like a maniacal totem pole carving.

"Whoa... of course he did. Larry is amazing. Hey, can I get a cig off of you?" Babs pushes herself forward onto her knees and reaches out a hand.

"Sure, here." Annie hands the case and lighter to Babs, waits for her to pluck a cigarette out with two thin fingers, then snap the case shut, light up, and hand everything back. "I mean, we got the full star treatment back there. There was champagne, and chocolate covered strawberries, and sushi. The couple of rooms we were hanging out in were sorta ratty, but..." she grinned, "that made sense, considering."

Babs felt her back relax into the smoke. "So who was this guy?"

"You are an impatient little monster, arentchya?!" Annie taps the cigarette along the edge of one of her art deco ashtrays arrayed on the small, mirrored table next to her chair. "I'm *getting* to that. So we had fun. I didn't know who any of the people were backstage. But Larry obviously knew one guy. Someone he sells to. I don't remember even what he looked like. I mean, it was like a parade of matching Glam dolls, all gussied up, looking for attention. They all had the same big, shellacked hairdos. And they all wore the same skinny black pants and lacy black shirts. And all that big fake jewelry, ick. I was the only person there in *style*, my dear."

Annie rolls her shoulders and peers out at the brightening sky outside. "Jesus, it's late. Or early."

Babs takes another drag off her ciggy and tries to settle down, hoping the story is going somewhere soon.

"Fuck, I didn't have any idea who anyone was. Obviously, we were backstage with one of the bands while the other band played. And then probably the other band while the other band played. People kept coming in and going out. But I had my little glass of champagne and Larry tooted me up in the bathroom, so it was a party." Annie smiled in satisfaction. So happy with the way the story was coming out, she could hardly wait to tell a crowd of listeners.

"Anyway, blah blah blah. Long night, hanging out, doing

lines, drinking bubbly. Then this one guy- Larry's guy who got us in- walks up with his arm around this shy looking skinny blonde dude and introduced him to us. I guess he wanted to meet me." She grins hard again. Babs sees that scary totem face, eeee.

She stubs her cigarette out into the ashtray by the stereo. "So...?"

"That, my dear little Babylon, was the bass player from Ratt. He loves Marilyn almost as much as I do. We started chatting, then did some lines, then started making out. He asked if he could accompany me home. Hah, I said sure, why not. So I told Larry I was heading, we slipped out, got into a *limousine*, and made out all the way back here." She reaches up to trace her finger along an imaginary line on the window behind her.

"Look, I'm as surprised as you look right now. I haven't slept with a guy in about four years?" Annie purrs. "But he was hot in a femme way. If he'd a been a chick, I'll bet he'd still be here, all wrapped in mama's arms."

Babs grins now, she gets it. "Oh right... take what you can get, and make it work for ya. I guess." The next words are out of her mouth before she can stop herself. "But he didn't get you off, so you chased him down the street with DiMaggio?!"

As soon as the last words are out of her mouth, Babs realizes her mistake. Annie won't appreciate her having been witness to all of that. Or finishing her story for her— one or the other: either way, unwelcome. She sucks in a quick breath.

Annie sits up a little straighter. "Fuck, you heard all of that? Of course you did. Little girl, this is not your story to tell." She rolls her shoulders again. "That's why I don't have roommates."

Annie sighs. "But yes, that is *indeed* what happened. He was a good kisser. I got turned on making out with him and feeling the mystery packet in his jeans on the way here in the cab. I mean, so much about this Ratt was feminine– his hair, his tiny hands, the way he dressed. Even getting all that gear off him and obviously, he's a boy underneath. Even that was femme somehow. And everything was *fine* until he wouldn't slow down and started taking off like a rocket, and – well, you heard right– the little fucker didn't get me off."

Annie plants one hand on each knee and pushes herself up to stand with a "Whoof!" She looks down at Babs still seated cross-legged on the floor. "You know, if you were more my type, I'd grab you and throw you in the bedroom, and make you make me cum right now." She winks at Babs. "Lucky for you you're not. My type."

Babs unlocks her jaw again and nervously laughs, "Yeah, heh. Great fucking story though. Sorry I was here, but I'm kinda glad too." Not waiting to see if Annie decides to do or say something else, Babs pushes herself up onto her feet and turns towards the kitchen doorway. "I'm gonna try to crash. Goodnight."

Annie takes a step away from the window which is now flooding the room with a faint yet painfully bright light for Babs' weary speed-soaked eyes. "Hey, I'm serious about the roommate sitch. I let you stay here a little while, but tonight just proves that little while is up. I'm gonna head to Berkeley for that show next week and want you out of here by the time I get back."

Babs' jaw locks up again. "Ummm... but, where...?"

"I don't care. Not my problem. Let's say Sunday. That gives you a whole week and a half to figure it out." Annie walks towards her bedroom, stops at the arched entrance, and spins to look at Babs. "No guff. I've been generous and I'm tired of giving too much away. To you, to Shelly, to that Ratt fucker."

Babs thinks to herself 'don't say it'. What she really wants to say is 'You don't give a fucking thing to anyone!' She's trying her best to make sure that what she's thinking doesn't show on her face.

But evidently, not well enough. Annie sighs. "I know you think I'm a bully. I'm not. I'm a big softy and people take advantage. Just like Marilyn. People use me but they're not gonna use me up." She suddenly balls her fists up, leans forward, and bellows, "DON'T FUCK WITH BLONDIE!"

As Babs flinches and steps back into the kitchen, Annie grabs the pocket doors to her bedroom and slams them closed. One bounces back open slightly, reverberating for a moment. Then Annie pulls it shut again with a loud crack.

'Don't fuck with Blondie' repeats Babs to herself. 'Is that you, or me, now?'

"The coldest winter I ever spent was a summer in San Francisco"
– **Mark Twain**

Death in the City

1

Amy punches her foot hard onto the pavement, throwing her shoulders into the pump and push action. She's skating hard and has her favorite rhythm going now. Plant foot, push off, fingers hands arms almost pulling her along, like threading a needle. Plant push glide. Plant push glide. The sound of her wheels chewing up the street, flying and fast, gives her such a rush. This is her favorite time to lose herself in the here and now of the world she knows.

Passing a blur of storefronts along Haight, she leans into her board and hard turns left across traffic down Clayton Street, allowing herself to coast a bit before picking up speed again with another push off. She sees- or thinks she sees- Max and Henry out of the corner of her eye. But she's on a mission now, going somewhere fast and hard, and she doesn't have time to stop and check out what they might be up to.

Amy swerves slightly to avoid getting too close to a

mother pushing a baby stroller across a driveway halfway down the street. Plant push glide. Skating is often like a real-life video game, except when you wipe out, it's not always so easy to get right back up on the board and keep going. Especially the way Amy skates. Tough and fast and hard. She owns these streets on her board. She loves the breeze across her face, and the threat of nearly going down every so often. Fucking thrill of a lifetime, each ride.

At the corner of Clayton and Waller, Amy checks the street for traffic, then leans back and allows herself to surf out into the middle of the street, both arms raised shoulder height, balancing her flight. Her right hand points where she wants to go, leading her there. Then she shifts, and plant push glides across the street, aiming for the church at the corner.

There's a small group of punks gathered outside. The Food Bank must not be open yet. A few of them turn and watch as Amy aims for the curb, then leans into her right front foot on the board, and twisting her left foot down and hard to that side, forces her ride to a sliding screeching halt. Quick step on the tail and flip the board up into her right hand. Amy tucks it under one arm and approaches the cluster of ragged looking kids gathered together in front of the angel steps, smoking.

"Hey Mouse, what's going on?" Amy smiles at the lanky, gorgeous brunette wearing her hair up in some kind of 1940's rag-do, like she always does. Are those curlers in her hair?

Mouse lives behind Pat's, in a studio apartment over behind Petrini's Market on McCallister Street, on the other side of the Panhandle. She and her boyfriend Rick shack up with their teensy black kitten, Smoke, and huge never-ending piles of vintage clothing that Mouse repairs and wears. That's her thing. That, and the doubles strip dancing she specializes in at the Garden of Eden. She used to dance for the Mitchell Brothers, but Rick didn't like the way one of the managers watched Mouse too closely, so he had her quit and move her acts over to the GoE.

Now Rick 'manages' Mouse. Every night she works, he escorts her on the bus downtown. And at the end of every shift, he's there to make sure she's in one piece and they stop for fries and malts before heading back to the apartment. Unless there's a show Rick wants to hit up. Then he'll walk around the show, asking everyone he sees, "What time is it? What time is it?" over and over again all night until it's time for him to meet Mouse. He leaves the show, walks or takes the bus to the Garden, and if it's not too late, Mouse and he head back to wherever- the Mab, the Tool and Die, the Deaf Club, the Sound of Music- to catch the last band finishing up.

Mouse laughs and reaches her long arms around Amy's tiny body for a fierce hug. She likes this little punkette something fierce. Amy is probably the least self-absorbed person Mouse knows in The City, and she loves her for her fresh naiveté. Plus she always smells good. Amy is one of the few punkettes Mouse knows who showers regularly.

"I'm doing alright, Aims. What's up?"

Amy blushes. Being the focus of Mouse's attention is like having more than one set of eyes on you. She has an effortless movie star grace, and always all dolled up like she is, there's always an audience around Mouse.

"I'm fine. Hey, gotta cigarette? I haven't eaten in a couple of days and I need something to take the buzz off until they open up. Isn't it twelve yet?" She peers around the small group to peek at the door behind them.

Mouse pulls a crumpled pack of Old Golds from the pocket of her gabardine chinos. "Here, take two." She hands the cigarettes to Amy. Amy taps one, then two cigarettes from the pack, "Hey, this only leaves you with...three cigs. That ok?" She waits. Mouse shakes her head, while touching one of the curls that has come loose from her scarf. "Of course.

You know I'm rollin'." Amy grins that lop-sided grin of hers, finishes tapping out the two cigarettes, and thumbs the matchbook from where it is nestled, flap out, inside the cellophane wrapper. "Thanks Mouse..."

She places one cigarette behind her ear, and lights the other, slightly hunching her body around the flame from habit, even though there is no breeze. She slowly releases that first thin stream of smoke. "How's Rick?"

Mouse steps back against the angel mural along the church steps and leans against the wall. She rests one foot against the wall, and placing the cigarettes back in her pocket, looks up at the wedge of sky along Waller. "He's good. He's having one of his days, so I left him at the apartment with a stack of comics. You know how he gets. Hey, wanna 'escort' me to work tonight? That will make him feel like he's still taking care of me. He trusts you."

Rick has something going on in his head that affects his ability to make quick decisions. He doesn't handle change well either. One of his 'days' usually looks like Rick making a mistake- dropping an egg while making breakfast- or saying the wrong thing in front of a group of friends who then laugh- and then he just can't let go. He agonizes over what he did wrong, how *stupid* he is, why couldn't he have just done the thing right, or said the right thing, or not said anything at all...

Mouse knows how to make things right. She makes a pitcher of grape Kool-Aid, piles a heap of Cheesy Peanut Butter Cracker packets onto a plate, and sets him up in bed with their kitty Smoke and a stack of comics. Usually, by the end of the day, he's forgotten all about whatever set him off, and he's ready to head out into the world again. Though sometimes not. Sometimes, she'll come back to the apartment from Pat's, where she's gone to gossip a bit, or from thrifting all afternoon, and he'll be sitting on the floor, cross-legged, hunched over with his head in his hands, moaning... She's seen the man cry, and that breaks her heart.

She thinks today might be one of *those* days. Rick had awakened this morning, jumped out of bed and promptly kicked Smoke across the room. It was an accident, but she just couldn't tell him that. He couldn't hear it. Smoke seemed alright- skittish at first, and maybe a little bruised? But she'd settled right down, turning into the purring machine that she is, once Mouse picked her up and snuggled her a bit. So who knows what she'll come home to after she hangs for a bit with her friends here at the soup kitchen.

Even though Mouse makes good money at the Garden, she

comes to the soup kitchen just to catch up with friends, since most often, she works nights when they're all at this show or that. Sometimes she helps organize donations and putts together the boxes of food that folks pick up on their way out the door after a hot meal.

Amy flips her board up on one end and leans on it. "Of course! I was gonna head to the Mab tonight anyway, so I can just detour around thataway with you first." She looks up as the small group shuffles away from the door a bit. "Hey, they're opening, yay…"

The small group shuffles in through the large door with the big hand lettered yellow sign saying Haight Ashbury Food Program. One of the kiddos- that's what Amy calls the ever-shifting gaggle of kids who come and go around The City - stoops and wedges the small triangle wood piece into place beneath the door, then stands and kicks it a bit so it holds firm. Amy and Mouse go around him and head inside.

The smell of fresh baked bread hits them as soon as they round the small vestibule and enter the large seating area filled with long tables and a mix of benches and chairs. Amy inhales deeply. Fresh baked bread reminds her of her mom…

The girls head straight for 'their' table, to the right and by the small bank of windows that peer onto the street, farthest from the door and the serving area along the back wall. Amy pulls the bench out slightly from the wall and slides her board upright between the two. She nudges the bench over a bit so it holds the board up firmly in place. "Oh God, they made bread today…"

"Actually, they had a class yesterday," one of the kiddos says. This one with the requisite stained, torn white t-shirt, shredded flannel shirt wrapped around her waist, and jeans so torn they're more string than material. Also wearing the new standard: shaved head with a small row of fringe across her forehead. "They taught us how to make hobo bread. Cool?!"

Mouse shakes her head. "What's hobo bread?"

Standard fringe looks from Amy to Mouse, the surprise on her face spreading from the 'o' of her mouth to her widening eyes. "Oh, sorry, uh, I didn't know you were with her."

Mouse laughs, then raises both hands and shrugs, "No that's fine. I'm Mouse, and this is Amy. What's your name?" And then, "And what's hobo bread?"

The kiddo smiles. "I'm Jasmin. I just got here this week."

She grins wider, obviously happy to be in The City, happy to be included in this conversation. She turns and points at two other kiddos slouched over a table nearby. "That's Horse and Ronnie. We've been camping in the park!"

Amy notices they all have bundles- thin blankets rolled up and tied with rags that double as straps. Jasmin's bundle has a ceramic cup hanging off one end, and a kerchief bulging at the other end, filled with, what, fresh socks? Another torn band t-shirt? Oh kiddos... "And...? What's hobo bread?" Amy fakes exasperation, rolling her eyes.

"Oh, sorry! It's this bread that you make when you're a hobo, you know from back in the depression days?" Amy nods and Mouse purses her lips slightly, like a professor listening to a class report. "So you make the filling, the dough part, first. Then you grease a big empty tin can. Like from tomato sauce? Then you put the filling inside the can. Put a piece of tin foil over it and put a big rubber band over that."

Amy has to interrupt. "Tin foil? I think that's also from the 'depression days'. I'm pretty sure it's aluminum foil they use now." She smiles encouragingly even while correcting Jasmin. Don't want to scare her. She already looks like she doesn't know whether to keep talking or scamper away. Ah, kiddo. Even though Amy is only probably a few years older than Jasmin, she's already spent enough time on the streets here to be one of the old-timer generation of street punks-those who can impart their street wisdom to the revolving door of kiddos coming and going every day.

Jasmin half smiles nervously. "Right. So *aluminum* foil. And the rubber band. Then you boil a big pot of water and put the can in that. When it floats, the bread is ready to come out. Then you let it sit a while- I don't remember how long." Jasmin turns to her friends. "Hey Ronnie! How long is the hobo bread supposed to wait before you can take it out of the can?"

Ronnie, the slightly taller mirror image of Jasmin-uniform, fringe, bedroll- turns partway on the bench where she's sitting, facing away from the trio. "I think it's about an hour. Right, Horse?" She turns back to the third kiddo, a faintly dusky skinned skinhead with no fringe, repeat uniform, bedroll, and dirty face. "Yeah, at least one hour." Both Horse and Ronnie watch politely while their friend finishes telling her story.

"Yup, one hour. Then you take the tin- *aluminum*- foil off the can, slide a knife around inside the edges, and shake it upside down to shake the bread out. Onto a plate. And it comes right out! Bread!" She rocks back on her heels, satisfied she's successfully spoken to these ultra cool, seasoned punks. I'm doing this! She thinks to herself.

Mouse touches the scarf on her head, making sure all her curls are still in place. "Well, that's amazing. I had no idea you could do that." She looks at Amy. "Did you?"

Amy grins lopsided, looking at Mouse and then turning to the kiddos. "No, that's really cool. Is it good? I guess we'll get to try some?" The smell of hot green beans and something tomato-y has now filled the room. Lunch is being served, and Amy is starving.

Jasmin cracks her knuckles. I think they said something about anyone who wants some can take some home. We made a *bunch* yesterday." She edges around the table to reach her friends. "Ok, well I'm gonna go eat with Horse and Ronnie. Nice meeting you."

Good manners, thinks Amy. Wonder how long that will last. "You too. Thanks for letting us know about that. Enjoy your lunch," she smiles again and places both hands on her stomach. "Ugh, I'm starving. Let's eat."

2

Amy removes her faded graying sweatshirt from around her waist and lays it across the two seats where she and Mouse plan to sit. They both walk around the tables to get in the short line that is moving briskly past the food window at the back of the room. The trio of kiddos watches them, and tries to figure out what to do with their blanket bundles. Should they drape their plaids across the benches like Amy and Mouse did?

Amy grabs a tray and helps herself to a spoonful of green beans, then another. She loves the taste of overcooked beans. Next to that are three trays of lasagna. Amy takes a thin slice. When she's been high for as long as she was this past week, her stomach can't, well, stomach rich foods. Unless it's a little bit of ice cream. Most of the time, she picks at some overcooked veggies or gets a small order of Chicken McNuggets from Mickey D's at the end of Haight, or she'll make cinnamon toast and fill up on a few pieces of that. Lasagne though. Maybe she can suck the sauce off the noodles? The thought of cheese makes her stomach roil.

Mouse wrinkles her nose at the overly cooked green beans. Sigh. Ok, she'll have a small piece of the lasagna, but she can't afford to get gassy tonight. Tonight she's on stage, not just in one of the booths. She hates when she gets that bloated feeling, and it's a turn off if one of the dancers farts on stage. So nope, no dead beans. Anyway, she can make a salad when she gets home, see if Rick wants to eat with her before she has to go through her bag and make sure she has everything for tonight.

They carry their nearly empty trays back to their spot and arrange themselves along the bench. Mouse takes a bite of lasagna. Actually it's pretty good. They always surprise her here, these old hippies. Amy picks at the lasagna, then spears as many green beans as she can onto her fork and shovels them into her mouth.

The room is bubbling with conversations and the sounds of chewing. The line to reach the food window snakes out the door, and punks are standing around, holding trays, and waiting for a seat to open up. The babble-on of hungry, smelly kids eager to talk to friends they haven't seen in a while balloons and fills the room, competing with the mighty scent of lasagna, beans and bread, making Amy sweat.

"Hey Amy, I've been wondering. Would you ever want to make some big money dancing?" Amy looks up at her friend in surprise, a fork full of green beans hovering over her plate.

"You know I do these doubles dances, right?" Amy nods. Mouse puts her fork down and pushes the tray slightly away. "The girls I dance with, we work in these isolation booths. No-one can touch you. And because the lights are on us, you don't really see who's behind the windows."

Amy puts her fork down and pushes her tray away too. "Windows? I thought you were on some kind of stage."

"That's different. For doubles, there is this room that is kind of circular, with a door at one side where we go in and out, but none of the *clientele* can enter. *They* go into these little booths arranged around the room, you know, through a curtain at each booth entrance. They get settled in, feed coins into the slots at the front of the booth, and the window covering raises up, so they can see us in the room, doing our thing, but we can't see them."

Amy toys with the lip of her serving tray. "Huh, that's sorta like a cow being led to slaughter. There's all these series of chutes and doors that prevent you from seeing what's up ahead so you don't get flustered."

Mouse leans in, mock frown upon her pretty brow, "Did you just call me a *cow*?!"

Amy inhales quickly and coughs as a fleck of spit catches at the back of her throat. "No! I mean... just how the set-up is that you just told me about. The little booths, not being able to see..." She cracks her knuckles and shyly looks up at her friend. "Oh... Mouse!" Amy slaps Mouse lightly on the shoulder. They both giggle.

"I *know* you were kidding, Aims. So what do you think? We could work up a story. You name it. Eve and Eve in the Garden of Eden, for one. Use boas as prop snakes. Or I don't know, Mary-Anne and Ginger from Gilligan's Island..."

"Why is there a story? Don't you just dance and get all sexy with each-other?" Amy blushes. Is she seriously considering this?

"You create characters inside a story so that the clientele remembers *your* story. They remember *you*, not just some tits and ass shaking and writhing around. Hopefully they like the story- *and you* - and come back for more of that."

Amy nods, "Yeah, ok I get it." She scratches the back of her hand. She's starting to feel itchy and wants out of here- too much noise, conversation, chaos, too many smells. "I don't think I could do that though. I'm maybe too shy..."

Mouse barks a short bright little laugh. "*Maybe too* shy?! Oh Aims. You are the poster child for shy. We need to put a picture of your ego on a milk carton." She pokes one finger at Amy's emaciated right bicep. "You would have to cover up any track marks though. Lots of girls wear these fun opera gloves that do the trick."

Amy pushes her tray away, "Oh *that's* why you shoot between your toes? I didn't know. I thought it was some kind of 1940's thing..."

Mouse nods, and giggles again, "So will you please... anyway, think about it? I like the Mary-Anne and Ginger story."

Amy leans in quickly, lowering her eyes and voice, "Did you hear that?" She tilts her head slightly to her left. "I don't know who said it, but someone just said something about a dead body – some kiddo- being found in a dumpster off Divisadero." She whips around, "Excuse me. Did someone just say something about someone being found dead in a dumpster?"

One of the nameless kiddos at the table behind them speaks up, "Yeah. I heard it was Jen, that rat-punk from Oregon."

They both speak at once. "Do you know what happened?" "I don't know what happened. Just that her body was found."

The tables around them stop talking, silverware poised mid-air over trays of food. Someone speaks up. "What did you just say? Jen's dead?"

The nameless kiddo coughs lightly into his hand. "Yeah, I heard it from my friend who listens to the police scanner. He didn't know if it was the same Jen, but has anyone seen her for the past couple of days?" He looks around at some of the faces watching him.

People look to one another, the question in their eyes and on their lips. "Did you...?" One tall-ish thin mohawk leaning against the wall pushes away, "This is *bullshit.* Jen's not dead! She was just at our place..." He turns to his friend against the wall next to him, who shrugs unhappily, trying to count the days.

Amy looks back at the kiddo seated behind her. "I don't know Jen, though I think I know who you're talking about. Is she that tiny little thing with a big mop of orange hair that always sort of covers her face? She wears a lot of lacy scarves?"

The kiddo nods, yes that's her. He speaks up. "Look, I'm not sure it's her. But I can ask my friend if he heard anything else."

Mouse speaks up, calmly looking around the room. "That might not even be her real name. Wasn't she calling herself Jenny Jujube?" A few heads nod, and murmers of 'yeah, that's her' come from around the room. "Let me ask my housemate, Pat. She gets word from a friend of hers who's a cop. If she can tell me more, I'll post something here on the board, ok?"

Someone sniffles, and the room shuffles around. There are nods and the din of trays and silverware in motion once again. Mouse looks at Amy. "Let's get out of here. I want to see if Pat is up and coherent, and I need to spend a little time with Rick before I get ready for work. You coming?"

"Yeah, can you watch my board? Let me grab that." Amy stacks Mouse's plate and silver with her own and shuffles her own tray atop Mouse's. She quickly moves to the side of the room, where she scrapes both plates, deposits the plates and silver in their respective bins, and places both trays atop the small pile near the trash.

Mouse grabs Amy's board with both hands and carefully hands it to her little friend, who tucks it under her arm as they head for the door. "Oh wait, my sweatshirt." Amy jogs back to their bench, where the Mohawk has already taken a seat and hands Amy her hoodie.

She thanks the Mohawk, and backs away from the tables, so she doesn't swing around and smack someone with her board. "Let's roll."

The girls step outside into fresh air and a sunnier day. They pause on the sidewalk outside the Food Bank. Amy shakes her head. "Fuck. That's grim. Would anyone know how to get in touch with Jen's folks? If it's her?" She thinks of her folks, and her brother back home, if anything happened to her.

Mouse touches one of her curls, patting it back into place. "I'm sure the cops know how to do all that. Fuck. It *is* grim." She looks up the street in the direction they both need to go. "You wanna come with?" Knowing her friend likes to skate hard whenever there's something to ponder, and this is something to ponder for sure.

Amy lowers her board to the sidewalk and places one foot on it as she straightens up. She ties her sweatshirt around her hips so the Anarchy sign neatly covers her rump and signals greetings like a flag in her wake. She dips her head slightly towards the board, then looks up at Mouse.

"No, thanks. I've gotta skate this off. Um, what time do you want me to stop by to escort you to the Garden?" She rolls the board back and forth a little, revving up to hit the street.

"Oh right. Come over at 4:30. Oh Aims…" Mouse folds her long arms around her friend's tiny shoulders and hugs her close, lightly dipping Amy off her board. Mouse releases her, "Ok, go skate tough. But promise me you'll skate safe?"

Amy grins her lopsided grin. "I can't exactly promise *that*. But I'll be a good girl." She plants her foot on the board and swivels it in the opposite direction from home. "See you later."

Mouse places both hands on her hips and stands with her feet apart. "Ok. Just... be safe. You little monster."

Amy carefully plant push glides to the edge of the sidewalk then maneuvers onto the street. "Fuck... grim. See you later." She turns away from her friend and starts her hard skate towards the end of the street, where she'll figure out which way to go from there.

"San Francisco is a golden handcuff with the key thrown
away."
— **John Steinbeck**

Mine All Mine

1

Shelly opens her eyes with effort, her lids gummed shut
with sleep. "Uhhhhhh..... wha the fuh...?" Even though the
room is dim, thin shafts of light from the doorway shard
her brain into splinters, owwww... She tries to roll over onto
her side but discovers she can't. Her arms are trapped,
somehow, extended above her head. She blinks her eyes
apart, no matter the pain.

The first thing she sees are her wrists shackled to a pair of
handcuffs attached to the bed frame above her. "Oh..." She
remembers faintly, something about one thousand and one
nights, a sheik, and she his sex slave... "Fucking Omar."
She pulls down against the cuffs a little, to see how snug
they are. They're tight.

She stops pulling and lies back, closing her eyes again. The
room smells of funk- days of pungent sex and sweat and
rich incense. The satin sheets are gritty and nasty beneath
her. The more awake she feels, the less painful the light

seems. The less her head splits, the more she realizes how fucked she is.

Shelly turns her head to look at first one, then the other cuffed hand again. Her arms are half numb, half tingling. She needs to get out of this. How did she allow herself to get here, in the first place?

Omar had been charming at first. All roses, and champagne, fancy dinners and gifts. Stories of his family back home, and how she was going to be his princess when he brought her home to meet them. She'd first met Omar through one of her dealer contacts. Shelly had seen how the streets were changing. More druggies were opting for downers, pills, and H, so she'd decided to look into expanding her line from speed and sometimes coke to include everyone's all-time downer fave, Heroin.

She'd asked her contact. They said they knew just the guy and arranged a meeting between them at a neutral house. Shelly knew the place well and thought she knew the contact- Marco- as a friend, so she happily went to the appointed meeting place.

Marco had set up a small table in his parlor with fancy tea things: elegant sugar tongs, little cookies, and milk or lemon- all arranged quite prettily on gilt-edged china and a delicately flowered tablecloth. A tall, handsome, well-dressed man with jet black hair stood when she entered the room. She held out her hand in greeting, but he pursed his lips and placing his hands behind his back, bowed slightly at the hips instead. His eyes flashed and seemed to record everything about her.

After they made their introductions, Marco asked them to be seated and poured them each a cup of tea. Sugar, milk and lemon were offered, as well as the cookies. Marco explained Shelly's business, and what she was looking to do, then he dusted off his hands and went into the other room, leaving them to their meeting in private.

Shelly took a sip of her tea, and offered, "This is nice. Strange, but nice. Marco has never made me *tea* before." She waited. Nothing. Omar smiled slightly and continued to watch. He took a sip of his tea, and Shelly couldn't help but notice how feminine his hands were, lightly furred with hair as they were. They were pretty hands. And that gorgeous ring on the pinky of his hand holding his cup. It looked like antique gold, with a medium-sized blue-ish gem of some kind, and tiny figurines along the band. She leaned in to get a better look.

"Are those..?" She didn't want to point. They were tiny female figures, all holding the gemstone above their heads- tiny breasts, bellies and legs extending around the band to meet, presumably, at their feet in the middle on the other side of the ring. Omar had smiled then, revealing gorgeous, straight, clean white teeth in a confident smile. He placed the cup on the saucer and held up his hand for Shelly to inspect more closely.

"This is from my family. It is an old ring from my great-grandfather, passed down to my father's father, then my father, and then to me. I will pass it along to my son someday."

"Oh, you have a son?" Shelly sat back. This is a new sort of drug business. Hopefully they would get to that soon. Shelly needed to get home and weigh out some dime bags. She needed to dye her hair. She had some other things to do, and realized she needed to stop thinking about all that and focus. Maybe, when their business was done, she could ask if he could find her a ring like that too?

Omar smiled again- his lips and teeth a blend of disarmingly gorgeous and big bad wolf. Shelly felt that familiar electric twinge between her thighs. Nice.

"La la..." His accent was slight, almost formal in the slant of vowels to rigid consonants. "I intend to give this to my son *when I have a family* one day." He explained.

Shelly responded with a small, flirtatious smile. "Well then. Let's talk about what we came here to talk about first. Then we can talk about *that*."

Omar had laughed then, showing those gorgeous fangs, and tutted, before leaning in to consider what they'd come to discuss.

Once their business had been determined- what he carried, how often she could re-up, what the costs would be, and how they would exchange money for goods- Marco had sashayed back into the room. He'd been listening in and waited for the right moment to reappear all along. Shelly and Omar stood, and he followed her to the door, where Marco said something about being glad to bring them together. Shelly didn't really hear Marco's words, with those delicious eyes upon her.

They'd begun their dealings right away, and business had been good. Once a week, Shelly would meet Omar at Marco's with an envelope full of cash. Omar would place a small silk pouch of glassine bags on the tea table for Shelly, and another, smaller pouch directly into Marco's trembling hand. Most of the time, the product had been clean. None of that dirty shit from Mexico in tightly folded little colorful balloons for Omar. No, he dealt purely with Persian brown, ranging in color from a lovely light powdered tan sprinkled with grains of white and black to a rich, deep brown- like Omar's skin. Shelly began to associate the product with the man and began falling in solemn lust with both.

She'd always used her own products, but that was when she had dealt purely in speed and coke. She loved the luminous, bright and authoritative way those drugs made her feel: so clever and on top of the world. And while, sure, she knew a lot of her customers overused- didn't eat enough or sleep enough- she always made sure to take care of herself. She would snort a few lines of whatever she was carrying at the time, and then stop, come down, eat something healthy, and eventually fall sleep.

She figured she would do the same thing with this new stuff. That was about the time Omar had started wooing her. He took her to fancy restaurants downtown where he would smile and watch her intensely, ask her questions about herself and her family, and make suggestions about things they could do together next.

Soon, they began attending concerts- not shows at the Mab or Deaf Club with her brother and his friends- but classy, chi-chi concerts with orchestras and string ensembles. He started bringing her small gifts- roses, a diamond pendant, a luxurious red scarf, more roses. And then he suggested they dispense with meeting at Marco's. After all, the service had been rendered some time ago. It was time for them to move forward and move on.

Of course, Shelly trusted Omar. He was charming, and gorgeous. He wanted to *do* things for her. He'd begun to speak of introducing her to his family. And the waiting... he still had not touched her. Even when they dined out, he indicated the staff should help her with her coat. He held open the door for her, but never so much as held her hand to help her out of the cab. She ached in anticipation, in desperate desire for that gorgeous gift he was holding back.

She asked him to come to her apartment, but he'd said no, he preferred to meet her on more elegant terms. Now that she's lying here thinking about that, what didn't she hear? What did he mean by that? This?

So she'd taken a taxi to his apartment on Nob Hill. The fancy decent sized one bedroom in a quiet building, on a quiet street. It was so close to the Tenderloin, yet worlds apart. The first thing she'd noticed upon being ushered into his place was the silver-grey wall-to-wall carpeting. And the metal and glass furniture, all sharp angles and modern, the somber, dark artwork on the walls, and the view of the Transamerica building. Wow. So different than her decrepit two-bedroom place in the Fillmore, across the street from one of the City's most notorious projects. Her landlord had refused to put bars up on the windows and her brother Gabe kept needling her to move. Hm, maybe she could see herself in a place like this. Perhaps with this man?

Omar had led her to the dining room, offered her a chair and took her purse and coat. She sat, and noticing the lovely, polished silver tray set beside the single red rose in its glass vase, remembered the cash was in her purse.

"Omar! Can I get my purse back, please?" She held out her hand. He paused in the entrance to the hallway that most likely led to the bedroom, and slowly smiled. "No, that can wait."

She offered, "I'd like to get this over with first, and then we can do whatever you have planned." He had stopped telling her where they were going and what they were doing. He would just instruct her what to wear, how to do her hair, what lipstick to put on. Tonight was one of those nights.

He pursed his lips, "Ok Shelly, if you insist." He stepped towards her and laid her coat across the back of the chair at the head of the table. He then hung her purse over the corner of the chair and reached for her hand. Finally. She looked up at the deliberate, small smile creeping across his lips, and his glinting, dark eyes, then down at her hand in his, at last. He brushed his thumb across the back of her hand.

"Let's, how do you put it, get this over with first." He clasped her hand more firmly and pulled her to him. She stood, and felt herself glide towards him, staring all the while into those eyes. He pulled her into his chest, and stroked her languidly with his other hand, from the nape of her neck down the ridge of her spine. She wasn't breathing. Breathe... With one hand firmly on the small of her back, he pulled her closer. Then with the hand lightly holding hers between them, he touched her chin, tilted her face up, and leaned in to kiss her.

"Ouch!" He bit her! She tried to pull away, but he held on tightly, rubbing against her. She could feel him stiffen and oh, it turned her on. Ok, so this is how we do *this*... She thought maybe her lip was bleeding, but somehow maybe that turned her on too. She leaned back in.

Omar had taken control from that point on. He led her into the bedroom, undressed her, turned away while he undressed himself, then did things to her that she'd been wanting him to do for a long time now – even things she didn't know she'd wanted.

After they'd done *that*, he'd left her in a thrumming pool of buttery hormones there on the bed, left briefly, and returned with the silver tray, upon which was arranged a glassine envelope of dope, a small oval mirror, new single edged razor, and clean glass straw. He placed the tray on the bedside table, and asked, "Would you prefer to chase it?" Shelly shook her head no. She'd only snorted dope, enjoying the way it rolled up into her brain like a window shade, cascading down the back of her throat, between her shoulder blades, and down her spine. Besides, chasing the dragon produced that funny burning smell that got behind your eyes and permeated everything. She wasn't sure why, but it seemed *cleaner* to her somehow, snorting it.

He'd laid out two short lines for her and held the tray while she held her hair back and dipped over the mirror to snort them up. Then he'd lain down beside her while she nodded out, ritually touching her hips and belly and thighs as she dreamt.

Shelly realizes now that he never did dope with her. Ever. At first, she didn't notice. And then when she did and started asking Omar if he was going to get high too, he replied that he would rather enjoy *her* high. From those first days in his apartment snorting dope and all that controlled sex, to a few days? Weeks? Later, when he shot her up for the first time ever, preparing the spoon, tying her off, staring into her eyes until the moment when he drew blood and plunged the smack into her veins. Which changed how they did everything from that point on.

How and where they met, how she dressed, what he allowed her to eat, who he allowed her to see, when he allowed her leave. She was spending less time at home, less time doing business, less time with her friends and brother, doing anything *she* wanted to do. She didn't even know *what* she wanted to do any more, so how could she spend any time doing it?

2

Now, as she pulls at her hands gingerly in their cuffs, Shelly remembers when even *that* changed, and she ended up here. One morningafternoonnight- all the hours and days have run together- Shelly realized she hadn't heard her pager go off in some time. She found her purse, carefully tucked away in the black glossy Chinese armoire along one wall of the always darkened bedroom. She sat back on the bed and fumbled with the purse's zippered pocket until she grasped the pager. She pressed the button, again and again, but it wouldn't turn on. Not knowing exactly what she was looking for, she opened the battery cover, checked the batteries, and snapped the case shut again.

Leaving her purse on the bed, she dressed in her underwear and bra, and walked into the kitchen to hunt for new batteries. Omar was leaning against the counter, peering out at the city. He turned when he heard Shelly's feet lightly slap the tile floor, saw what she had in her hand, and narrowed his eyes.

Without even waiting for Shelly to ask, he stepped forward, took the pager from her hands, and placed it on the counter next to his coffee cup. Shelly started to ask, "Do you have any batteries?" but without speaking, Omar placed one hand over her mouth, wrapped his free hand around the wrist of her still-outstretched hand, and twisted her arm so she was forced to turn around and face the hall to the bedroom. She tried to say "What the hell are you doing?" but he clamped his hand more tightly over her mouth, hurting her.

Shelly began to struggle and tried to twist out of his grip, but he held onto her rigidly and compelled her step by step back into the dark room at the end of the short hall. Once in the bedroom, Omar forced Shelly face down on the bed, smashing her nose into the satin coverlet. He straddled her and pressing into her from behind, held both of her wrists taut with one inflexible hand. How had she ever admired those hands? He reached into the purse she'd left on the bed and retrieved the beautiful deep red scarf he'd given her at one of their lovely restaurant dates not so long ago.

Omar shifted his weight so that he leaned across Shelly, pinning her down with his body. Stretching her left arm away from her torso across the bed, he leaned onto his elbows and tied one end of the scarf tightly around her wrist. He pushed her body further up onto the bed, flipped her over, and looped the other end of the scarf over and through one of the headboard's thin slats, yanking her arm painfully in the process. Shelly started to scream, and Omar slapped her hard across the mouth.

She looked up at him, stunned. This wasn't the sexy role-playing they had engaged in before. This wasn't fun at *all*. She tried to wriggle out from underneath him. He slapped her again, twice, then leaned back and punched her across the jaw. She heard as much as felt her jaw crack, followed by a sudden, searing pain that burned across her back teeth, sinuses, and down one side of her neck. Tears sprang from her eyes. Shelly blinked them back and looked at Omar with a dawning awareness. This was a new game, and she didn't know the rules.

She tried to relax at first. Maybe this was just part of something bigger. Surely Omar would soften and become her chivalrous leading man again, sometime soon. So she kept quiet and went along. Just do what he wants, and when this is over, think twice about coming back.

But he never let her leave. He'd tied her remaining arm and both legs open in an X across the bed. And then he began to beat her. Randomly, a slap here, a punch there, a knee to her genitals once or twice, hard bites on her breasts that left angry red marks now fading to scabs. She remembers it all, and it all hurts.

Every so often, he would 'fix' her. Prep the dope, tie her off, and shoot her up. When the veins in her arms stopped cooperating, he began shooting the drugs into the veins in her hands and feet. She remembers a moment, something that happened sometime over the past few... weeks? Omar had just dosed her– she didn't even think of it as getting high anymore. He was keeping her *down* and weak. He'd just shot her up, and stretched out alongside her, like he used to. He began whispering in her ear, and running his hands down her body, squeezing a breast, gripping her thigh, none of it loving, none of it even sexy. All she felt was enslaved and powerless. She recalls what he spat in her ear, "Mine. All mine."

Shelly isn't entirely clear about what else he did to her. Was there sex? She's in so much pain, she can't remember. She doesn't think there was sex. She looks down at her body, and up again at her wrists, starting to figure this out. Her eyes snap back to her body. Her legs are untied. When did that happen? She's so addled by pain and drugs that she didn't realize until now that her legs are free... So how long has she been here? And what else hasn't she noticed?

Come on, she thinks to herself. Get your head into it. How can I get out of this? Bending one of her legs to push herself up slightly, Shelly leans into one shoulder, allowing her to inspect more closely her cuffed wrists. Right, she recalls, he switched from the scarf to handcuffs at some point. Both cuffs are attached to the top of the headboard, looped around one of the slats, and enclosed tightly around each wrist.

Shelly jiggles one arm, then stops, and looks towards the bedroom door. She listens for any sounds out there. Where is Omar? Does he know she's awake? Why isn't he here?

She leans back onto her shoulders, and folding herself in half, reaches both legs over her head and tries to kick at the slats. She adjusts herself on the bed and tries again. She makes contact, and feeling a surge of energy from the impact, tries again. She leans back, braces her head and shoulders, kicks. Brace, kick. Brace, kick. Her left wrist begins to throb. She braces and kicks again. Beneath the muffled blow of her foot hitting the headboard, she hears a small 'crick'. Uncertain how much longer she can do this, nor how much time she has, she braces and kicks desperately. Brace, kick. She stops, scoots over to her left a bit, then braces and kicks again, and there's the 'crick' again.

Shelly stops a moment and focuses on where the weak point might be, if there is one. Is something actually breaking or is it her imagination? She has to try again. Pressing herself back onto the bed, she folds up and kicks again, harder. Suddenly, the thin glossy black slat pops out of the headboard. Her arm abruptly goes slack as her wrist slides freely down the slat, cuffs and all, and falls to the bed. *Oh my God, now what do I do?! I've got to get out of here before he comes back!*

Shaking from fear and determination, Shelly turns over onto her right side and pushes herself up into a sitting position. And it really can't be this easy, because right there, on the bedside table, is what looks like a set of handcuff keys. She reaches for them, though her fingers are a little numb, so she fumbles with them at first. She pumps her fingers and shakes her hand- *shake it off!* Then grabs the keys and twists around to see if these are really all she needs. The key fits perfectly, turning and clicking and the handcuffs release: first the hand still cuffed to the bed, and then the freed hand still encased in the other, dangling cuff.

Ok, she's out. What now? Where are her clothes? Any clothes? She eases herself off the bed- *what if he's just in the other room?* Not thinking of the all the noise she'd made while kicking and breaking the headboard. Quietly, slowly, she steps over to the dark bulk of the armoire. She opens the door slowly and grabs the first thing she sees- a crisp white man's dress shirt. And underneath, her purse, laid neatly across the floor beneath the well-cut suits and somber ties. She grabs her purse and drops it on the bed. Looking into the armoire again, she swiftly scans the shelves for a sign of anything else that is hers- shoes? Pants? Anything? Never mind, this is enough. Shelly slips the shirt on, and grasping it closed over her now trembling body, picks up her purse and walks slowly, toe-heel, toe-heel, towards the hall.

There is no sign of Omar. The light is off in the bathroom, and she inches past that door. Before the end of the hall, she stops, trying to calm her shaking and slow down her breath. She wishes she could peek around the corner without anyone seeing her, but there doesn't seem to be anyone there, so she steps once, steps again, slowly reaching the end of the hall, where she can see into the dining area and kitchen beyond.

Still no Omar. Shelly feels like her knees are going to give out, she's shaking so hard now. She walks over to the front door, expecting some type of heavy-duty special lock system to have been installed. But no. She unlocks the double lock above the door handle, turns the doorknob, and steps out into the hall.

Certain Omar will appear from around a corner- in the hall or stepping out of the elevator- Shelly runs to the end of the short, immaculately painted and furnished foyer, pushes open the fire exit, and begins running down the stairs as quickly as she can. Her knees tremble so violently they buck. She breathes in short, sharp jagged bursts of air. One flight, two flights, three. She has to sit down. *No!!!* Shelly forces herself to move, one shaky step at a time, down the fourth flight of stairs, to the building lobby doorway.

She's terrified as she pushes the door open and walks into the lobby with its ornate round wood table topped by a vase full of tastefully arranged colorful flowers. Past the neat row of brass mailboxes and the marble-topped side table beneath them bearing stacks of mailers and business cards. Towards the front door, that beacon luring her towards freedom from this loathsome prison.

Shelly loops her purse strap over one arm, and buttons the dress shirt as she steps up to the door. She counts one, two, three, and she's outside, and it's cold, and daytime. Morning? Evening? She can't tell. The street is radiant in that timeless, luminous San Francisco fog. *Now what?* She looks both ways along the sidewalk, making sure that Omar isn't walking towards her, even now.

Propelling herself against the wall, Shelly walks as quickly as her quaking, near-collapsing legs will allow, to the end of the street. One block further, and there is a small corner grocery. With no real plan in mind beyond *keep walking*, Shelly crosses the street, makes her way down the next block, and enters the store. She flinches as she looks to make sure Omar isn't there too.

The store owner glances briefly at her, then pays more attention as Shelly walks right up to the counter. "Do... you have a phone I can use? Please?" The owner begins to shake her head, no. But Shelly places both hands on the counter. "Please... I'm in trouble, and I need to call for help."

"Lady, are you alright? You want me to call the police?" Now the store owner is concerned, a crease furrowing her tan brow.

Shelly shakes her head no. "No, I need to call someone. Please?"

The owner shifts the phone from the far side of the register to the wider counter section in front of Shelly and spins the phone around to face her. She cracks a smile briefly in thanks, and rapidly punches in her brother's phone number, thinking *I hope he's home.* As the phone rings, once, twice, Shelly glances up at the plastic clock on the wall above the owner's head. 5:40. PM. This store wouldn't be open that early in the morning.

"Hello." Not a question. That's the way Gabe answers the phone. "Gabe!!! It's me, it's Shelly. Are you busy?"

She hears a quick suck of air at the other end of the line. "Shelly? Where the fuck have you been? I've been calling you and stopping by your place for weeks. Fuck, everyone's been asking *me* where you are for their fucking drugs.

Where are you?"

One of her knees gives, and she catches herself with one elbow across the counter. The store owner starts to reach across to help her, but Shelly waves her off. "I'm on Nob Hill. At..." She looks to the doorway, then back to the store owner. "Where are we?"

The store owner says, "Hyde Street." Shelly holds her hand out, "Yes, Hyde and...?"

"Washington."

Shelly smiles thinly. "Washington. Can you come get me? I'm in trouble. I mean, I'm not *now*, but um... I was handcuffed... I was a prisoner. I just broke out of his place and ran down the street. I'm not even wearing anything. Well, I'm wearing one of his shirts, but I couldn't find my clothes. Can you come get me?"

Gabe explodes, "Fuck, are you Ok? That FUCKER. I'm gonna KILL him. I'm going to hunt him down and I'm going to KILL him. Ok, I'll be right there. Don't move." He drops the phone and the line goes dead.

Shelly mumbles something and hands the phone back to the store owner. As she fumbles in her purse for a cigarette and finds none, her thoughts stray back to that "Mine, all mine..." She thinks Omar must have said that more than once. The words keep coming back to her. She leans against the counter and whispers out loud, "Not anymore, motherfucker."

The store owner looks at Shelly quizzically, "Excuse me, miss? There's no need for that language." Shelly looks up, "Oh no! I didn't mean *you*! I'm sorry. There was a man... and he hurt me. I was just thinking out loud... what I would say to *him*. I'm so sorry." She tries to smile convincingly, but her jaw hurts, her neck hurts, her arms hurt, *everything hurts.* "I'm sorry."

The store owner looks confused and lays one hand on the phone. "Should we call the police?"

Shelly thinks, then looks into her purse again to see if her wallet is there. "No, thank you. Or maybe, yes? What I want is some chocolate milk." She finds her wallet and looks up again. "Yes, please call the police. I'd also like some cigarettes- Superslims, hardpack, please."

Thinking to herself, 'This is mine, all mine', she walks to the back of the store to find the chocolate milk. She can wait for Gabe up front and figure out what to say to the police while she waits.

"San Francisco itself is art... every block is a short story, every hill a novel, every home a poem."
– **William Saroyan**

Mabuhay Nights

1

Val leans back against the cool, sweating brick wall. She raises one foot and plants it firmly on one brick, catching the heel of her boot along a slightly protruding edge. She places both hands in the pockets of her pleated chinos, a gift from Mouse. She pokes her elbows out slightly from side to side to carve out more space from the bodies against the wall around her. And she nods her head in time to the furious beat exploding from the stage nearby.

She loves this band, The Dead Kennedys. This is her fourth or fifth time seeing them play, every time here at the Fab Mab. Val gazes around the room, at the forest of bodies crushed together in front of the stage, at the punks less interested in the band and more involved in drug deals, flirting, and just being here tonight, spread out across the back of the room. There are a lot of people here tonight. The entrance out front was loaded with sweat and patchouli, a great packed crowd of people from all around the Bay Area, not just her gaggle of geese. She catches glimpses of punks she knows- the tip of a silvery Mohawk, her own artwork across the back of a hand-painted leather jacket, a quick profile covered in sweat and glee. There, then melted into the crowd gathered at the stage.

Val figures she'll hang here for a while- everyone knows this is her favorite spot. You can see the band- sort of- from this angle across the stage. You are close to the bathrooms and can watch the entrance. She hasn't seen Sophie or Amy yet, but she knows they'll be here. They all agreed to meet at the DK show tonight, she thinks she got the where and when part wrong though. No matter. She brought her travel kit. She has a few bucks she grabbed from her change jar for beer. Merde, she could hang here the whole show except for a quick trip to the bathroom for a refreshing bump.

Ah, there! She sees Max and Henry at the bar. And where Max and Henry are, Sophie will be close by. And where Sophie is, Amy will be in tow. She looks around the bar, over at the entrance, back to the crowd. *There*'s her Clits-sisters, Sophie with her five-day fuzz of goldish-red hair leaning over tiny, tough Amy, both rooted in their rapid, hand-signaling conversation.

Amy sees Val over at her spot and raises a hand in greeting. She holds up one finger, 'wait a sec', then points at Sophie and screws her finger round and round, 'crazy'...

Val grins. Amy says something to Sophie, who turns, and seeing Val, knocks Amy on the arm with one fist. They both head her way.

"Max and Henry are here! They're getting us beers!" Amy, rocked up onto her toes, screams into Val's ear. The band is loud.

Val nods yes, she doesn't like to screech at shows unless absolutely necessary. She reaches up with both hands and rubs the back of her friends' heads in greeting. Sophie grins around the pink bubble she is blowing, and Amy ducks her head, as always.

Actually, now's a good time to go for that refreshment she's been thinking about. "Hey! Can you stay here a sec?" She points to herself, then cocks her thumb to the back of the room behind her. "I'll be right back!" The girls both nod and step in to occupy the space she creates against the wall. Val pushes off and walks away. They know what she's heading back there to do. They know she'll share later on if one of them asks. That's part of their Clits-code. Share the goods, gals.

They both turn their attention to the band, which is just now launching into 'California über Alles'. Sophie wishes they had a single of this. She's heard through the grapevine that Tentacle might release something of theirs soon. She hopes it's this song. That growl and voice. That fucking attitude on stage. She loves these guys.

Sophie realizes that Henry and Max haven't left the bar yet. She sees them over there, looking around. As soon as she sees them, Henry sees *her*, nudges Max with his shoulder, and they both come over, offering room temperature, thin-tasting beers in plastic cups. Sophie grabs hers, kisses Henry on the neck, and takes a quick drink. It's hot in here and she's thirsty.

Amy smiles and nods at Henry and Max, and mouths 'thanks' as she accepts the sweating plastic cup from Max. She moves away from the wall to make room for Henry, who leans in over and around Sophie. Amy sighs a little bit. It's cool. Just sometimes… She steps back and raises her chin towards the bathrooms. "Be right back!" she screams at her friends, and holding her beer out in front of her, heads that way.

She passes Annie-X, all dolled up in black capris, a shiny jacket pulled screamingly tight across rolls of breast and fat, and clunky, colorful Hawaiian mules- the ultimate Annie-Marilyn get-up. They smile and mouth 'Hey' to one another. Amy likes Annie-X, no matter what some folks say about her. She took Shelly in after that crazy fucked up kidnapping. Took her in, nursed her back to health, even took care of her business and brought that back up to running speed too. 'Running speed', hah.

Amy moves around Annie's bulk, trying not to slosh her beer, and reaches the short line to the bathroom door. The noise behind her is growing louder. Someone has started a mosh, and people are getting tossed around and angry. As she strains to see what's going on at the stage, Annie steps in line beside her. Annie towers over Amy, sees what she's trying to see, and says, "Yeah! Some guy just threw up in the pit! Everyone is pushing him around in it, trying to mop it up with his *face*!" Annie loves a good fight.

Amy wrinkles her nose, "Ew..." and looks longingly towards the stage. She's so tiny, she can't really risk jumping into a mosh pit. She would definitely get hurt. Not that anyone would harm her on purpose, but that's just the way of things, the law of the pit. And even if there's no mosh, she's too short to see what's going on over other people around her. So either way, she can't go there.

The line moves up and the door opens to reveal space for one more inside the tiny women's bathroom. Amy knows the men's toilet is twice as big. There's a pisser in there *and* two stalls. There's only one functional stall in the women's, which makes for pant-wetting long lines later in the night. She looks up at Annie, who waves her in. "Go, go! I gotta pee!"

Amy steps through the poster-covered door just as the door to the stall swings open, forcing her to step back again. It's Val, who does a sort of double take once she sees who she almost beaned. "Amy! Fuck!" She grabs her little friend and pulls her into the bathroom and into the stall. Amy grins, that lopsided grin that Val adores. "Would ya like a *bump*?" She asks, saying the words lyrically, as though she's singing the offer in Italian, or Spanish, Amy can't tell.

She nods enthusiastically. This is one of her favorite show rituals. She'll do a line at the apartment, if she has any. Get ready for the show. Head there by bus or skate tough, depending on where the show is. Go inside, mingle, find her friends. And by then, she's always ready for something to bring everything into clearer focus and make it more *real*, more vibrant, more fun. Perfect timing, Val. She smiles in anticipation.

Val knows Amy's not into shooting up, and besides, Val doesn't like to share her needles. There's some bad shit starting to happen, people getting sick. And every use dulls your rig too quickly, so out with the mirror for Amy. Val sets everything up for her pal, dumping a nice little chunk of speed onto the mirror, then chopping it up into a fine sparkly powder. She arranges it all into two beautiful fat lines and offers the straw to her friend.

Amy concentrates as she takes the straw, bends to her task, and snorts up the sparkling crystal lines. She clamps the finger and thumb of one hand to each nostril and sniffs deeply, making sure to get all the love. Oh! It tastes a little chalky, but what the hell, it's doing its' job, either way. She hands the straw and mirror back to Val, who licks a finger, drags it across the mirror, and sticks it into her mouth. Brrrr, the taste of the drug sends chills up and down her spine. Val carefully places the mirror into a slit in the kit's flap, slides the straw into a small, webbed pocket, and the packet of speed and razor into a slightly larger pocket, then reverently rolls the whole kit up and places it neatly in the bag at her hip.

"C'est bien? On y va?" Val asks her friend.

"Perfect, merci!" They exit the stall, and maneuver around bodies to get to the mirror, where they splash water onto their faces and brush their hands back over their stubbly bare skulls. "Oh shit!" Amy turns back towards the stall, just in time to see a Hawaiian mule kick her nearly forgotten, now-warm beer across the floor. "It's ok. I didn't like that beer anyway." Sideways grin. Feeling good, and ready to head back into the crowded main room.

Behind the closed stall door, Annie grimaces, 'Fuck!' Her toes are wet, and she's ruined her favorite mules. She lifts her foot but can't see the damage. She knows the pad under her toes is wet. Maybe she can salvage it? She slips the shoe off, and grabbing a handful of toilet paper, dabs, then rubs at, the moistened pad. Maybe the beer didn't soak through? Annie grabs another few sheets of TP and folds them just so. Bending over her large belly and grunting, she places the TP flat against the bottom of her foot and slides the mule back on. That should work, she thinks hopefully.

Annie finishes her other business, then strolls out of the stall. Girls make way for her bulk, pushing themselves against the walls and into each other, out of her way. Annie turns her face slightly to the left, slightly to the right, making sure her hair and makeup are just right. She squints a little at her reflection in the cracked, graffitied mirror, *damn* the lights are so harsh in here. Annie gives herself one last luscious Marilyn gaze, then turns and bumps into the girls behind her on her way out.

Back in the main room, Annie thinks about which way to go. Over against the wall, near the Clits' spot? Closer to the stage? Left or right? Maybe upstairs? She's never been to the club upstairs, but she's heard they serve lumpia, all greasy and slathered in a sweet hot sauce, up there. No, that sounds disgusting right now. She pats her stomach, smoothing down the gold, shiny fabric of her jacket as best she can. Making her mind up, she heads to the right of the stage, where she can push her way up to the speakers, lean against them, and still see the band.

The crowd is swarming like bees now, throbbing and stomping in a confused swirl around the mosh pit, front and center of the stage. Another reason Annie likes to hang to the left or the right of the stage: she can't jump into the pit in her mules and can't risk messing up her makeup and hair in all the sweaty, lurching stage dives and chaotic crowd surfing.

Half the moshers have no idea what the fuck they're doing, anyway. Sure, the regulars at the center of the pit are running the show, aggressively mock marching around its growing circle. Just outside that mass, less certain punks try to jump in and join the arm-swinging, free-flying pit. Some make it. Some don't. Outside the pit, gagglers push in, shoved forward from behind, planting their feet so they aren't thrown into the reeling mosh. This section of the crowd tends to wear what Annie thinks of as costumes for their night out at a punk club. They have regular jobs, and houses and apartments where they pay rent and utilities. Fuck those people. They don't buy Annie's wares and they're in her way.

She forges a path around the jumping, wheeling crowd, past the heavy black support post in the middle of the floor to which a few audience members cling, to the ponderous speaker stack chained in place along the right-hand corner of the stage. Her left foot squish squish squishes every step she takes. Dammit. She tucks her large body behind the speakers and looks longingly back at the bar. She wishes she had a beer. Meh, Annie turns her attention to the band. They're really cranking it up now, though she can never understand how they go from 100% ON to even *more*... She wonders what happened to the guy who puked in the pit.

2

Carla thanks the doorman and smiles guiltily at the bouncer. She hooks the doorman up every time she comes to a show, so they always let her in for free. She walks to the end of the bar and peeks around to see if there's anyone she wants to hang with. Carla's not a big fan of massive, sweating crowds. She doesn't like all the distractions from her peaceful, happy high—what she considers her own personal Nirvana.

She decides to amble around the outer edge of the room first before making her way to the stage. She's not really here for the band anyway. She's hoping to see Red and find out if he knows about that kid who was found dead in the dumpster. Also, any update on what happened to Shelly.

Sometimes, Carla hears things, but she has to double check with another source to make sure she heard right. She's been known to hallucinate. *Was* Shelly really held captive for weeks? Did she really escape? Was there really and truly a body found in a dumpster? She knows Red knows what's going on around The City. He'll give her the straight news without the taint of exaggeration or gossip.

She walks around the back of the room towards the bathrooms, watching every face as she passes by. She sees one of her buying buddies- a punk she often sees coming or going from Shelly's or Annie's. She can't think of his name, but she stops and chats with him anyway. "Hey! How are you?!" She yells in the direction of his ear. He grins a huge wide-lipped, spit-flecked grin. He thinks Carla is a babe, and wonders if she wants to fuck him here tonight.

"Damn it's loud in here!" Carla screams. Spit-mouth nods, sure, anything you say. "Have you seen Red?!" She tries once more for some kind of verbal reaction. His grin falters, and his eyes get a sort of far-away look on them. Carla looks down. Did he just *pee* himself? Well, she can't tell, so she glances back up at his face. The grin is back in full force, complete with a shiny bubble of spit growing along the corner of his mouth. "Red?! Is *Red* here?!"

"Yuh, he's in the pit." Oh it talks, Carla thinks to herself. She stands on tiptoe to try to see over the crowd and into the pit up front. That won't work. She leans up into spit-mouth's ear one more time, "Ok thanks! I need to talk to him, if you see him!"

Suddenly, a short Neuro girl slides into place next to spit-mouth. Her hair is a mess, dreads and rats' nests, beads and feathers and some other shit hanging off it here and there. She's wearing a tight yellow tube top, lined with sequins and black feathers, and dirty, saggy black jodhpurs that end at her knees, lashed in place with an armory of belts at her hips and waist. She growls at Carla and wraps one hand like a talon around spit-mouth's arm.

"Get the fuck away from my man!" She screams into Carla's face, spittle flying like buckshot. These two are spit twins, what the fuck? Carla backs up, "What the *fuck*?! I was just *talking* to him, asking him a *question*!"

Angry Neuro Girl shakes her head, "Bullshit. I *saw* you flirting with him, bitch! Get the fuck *away* from him!" She rocks her head forward and back with every pulse of words. 'Bull' thrust, 'Shit' pull, 'I *saw*' thrust, 'You' pull, 'Flirting' thrust, 'With him" pull. Her dreads rock back and forth emphasizing her angry words.

Before Carla can reply, Angry Neuro's other arm shoots up and grabs the tiny ivory cross hanging from a slender silver chain looped through multiple holes in Carla's ear. She yanks *hard*, throws the cross on the floor, and stomps on it with her pointy Neuro horse-hair boot. Pain sears across Carla's ear. She reaches up to touch where the cross had hung just a moment ago, and her hand comes away slick with blood.

Carla stumbles back, and spit-mouth grabs Neuro's tube top and shoves her back against the bar. He starts screaming at his Neuro bitch, but Carla isn't interested in what he has to say. She puts her hand to her ear, and after quickly glancing at the floor beneath their feet to see if she can locate her favorite earring, she turns and rushes for the bathroom. "What the fuck!" She lobs across at the now-sobbing Neuro bitch. The small crowd that has closed in around them opens up to allow Carla through. They close in again behind her, watching and waiting to see what happens next.

Carla cuts to the front of the growing line for the women's bathroom. She uncovers her bloody ear to show the startled punkette waiting her turn why she needs access *right now*. The punkette says "Eeeew yeah, did you get in a fight?" Carla presses her lips together in reply and pushes into the bathroom. Inside, she excuses her way to the sink, revealing her bloody ear to everyone in line. At the sink, she rinses her hand, then rubs wet fingers over the bloody ear to see if that will clean it up. The silver chain dangles from the two other holes above the offended area, and... fuck. That bitch tore her ear. Where there had been a neat little piercing in the thick of her ear lobe, there are now two strands of flesh, bloody and fiery with pain.

Carla grabs a paper towel, moistens it, and places it gingerly around the torn lobe.

"You should put pressure on that." Someone behind her

offers. Carla pulls her mouth down in advance of the pain and holds onto her torn ear more firmly. That fucking *hurts*. Belatedly, she says, "Thanks."

A couple of voices trot out advice, ask what happened, offer to help. Carla's ears are ringing, and all she can think of now is that she wants to get high. She mumbles replies, "Thanks... yeah... no, I'll be ok... some bitch out there thought I was working her man. I *wasn't*!... I just asked him a *question*!"

The punkette who'd suggested pressure now suggests, "You want me to fuck her up? Do you know her?"

Carla turns away from the mirror to see who this would-be avenging angel is, face-to-face. She's tall, with spiky clown-red hair, a nose ring, and a generous sparkle in her eyes. Carla gets it. This gal just wants a fight.

"No, I can take care of it. Thanks though." She smiles, then grimaces, as her smile pulls at the tear in her ear. She gestures towards the stall behind them. "I need to..." The avenging angel steps aside, "Oh sure!" She bangs on the stall door. "Hey! Finish up in there! We have a wounded ghost who needs to use the can!" Carla smiles again, and grimaces right away. Fuck! Smiling hurts.

The toilet flushes, wait for it... no overflow, that's good, this time of night. The girl in the stall steps out, nervously buttoning her jeans and making for the door. She's one of those people here for a 'punk adventure night' and is afraid of everything she sees. Carla thanks her angel, and steps into the stall.

She latches the door behind her, gingerly trying to avoid touching the sticky metal lock or anything else. With her free hand, she grabs a few pieces of toilet paper, spits on them, and rubs one area clean on the top of the toilet tank. She pauses. Hmm, conundrum. She wants a hit, but every time she releases the pressure on her ear, it begins to throb and bleed. She can't prep or shoot up one handed, so... what a waste, but a few quick lines will have to do.

She holds onto the tissue pressed to her ear lobe with her left hand, and right hand now freed, dips into the small, mirrored cloth purse hanging at chest level from around her neck. Carla doesn't carry a mirror with her 'away kit', since she usually doesn't snort anymore. But she does have a razor, and a short handblown glass straw, in case she's feeling generous with friends who don't use needles.

She quickly taps out a small mound of sparkling crystals onto the spit-shined spot on the toilet tank, and pressing the rocks flat first so they don't skid or jump away, proceeds to carefully crush them. It's tricky, this process.

So much easier to shoot up! But head bent to task, she subdues the crystals into the powder-ish form that will suffice and lays them out into two short fat lines. She licks the razor- ah that cold, chemical taste- and places it back in the bag. She deftly locates the straw, rubs a bit of lint off the end with her thumb, and making sure she has a good hold on the tissue at her earlobe, dips her face to the drug. Carla sniffs the speed efficiently and skillfully, she thinks to herself. Ahhhhh!! That shard-like pain at the back of her skull and behind her eyes! She can feel the back of her throat constrict as the drug trickles down from her nasal passages. Not as lovely as that *bloom* you feel once the speed hits your bloodstream by needle delivery. But still, she appreciates this sort of kickstart and definitely feels the high coming on.

She moves the straw to her other nostril and snorts the second line. The metallic back-of-the-throat taste isn't as strong this time, but Carla is satisfied. She can feel the drug rushing through her veins already, forcing her heart to beat faster and sending sparkles around the edges of her vision. Time to pack it up and head back into the smelly masses, and maybe find Red.

Carla licks her finger, drags it across the spot where she'd lain the lines, and sucks at any picked-up residue. Brrrr... she shudders. She can hardly wait to get home and fix up properly later on. Maybe even mix a little H in for fun, see what comes from that?

She exits the stall, makes her way past 3 punkettes crowded around the sink to the mirror, where she test-pulls at the bloody tissue glued to her ear. It's fine for now. It makes Carla think of men who cut themselves shaving. She wonders how her ear will look after it heals.

As she pushes out from the bright bathroom into the pulsating dance hall, Carla observes the throbbing, roaring crowd with their wicked-looking clown-like faces. She hesitates, then wanders over to the back of the bar area, her focus split between searching the floor for her lost cross and not running into the people treading all around her. She spies sparkly things at the corner of her vision and turns towards them, only to have them disappear. Hey, she knows those sneakers... Her eyes travel from the dirty black and white Allstars up the black jeans-clad legs and black leather jacket she knows so well.

"Red!" He turns around and immediately smiles.

"My little sister! How you doing?!" How does he do that? Carla thinks. He's not even yelling but she can hear him clearly.

"I'm good, a little dazzly right now..." She rolls her eyes

around the room to show him what she means. Red frowns slightly, seeing her torn earlobe and the hasty first-aid job. "What happened here?" He raises his hand and cups it below her ear as though about to touch, but stops, as Carla flinches and says, "No! Don't! I just got it to stop bleeding!" She has to turn and shout towards Red's ear to be heard. He drops his hand.

"What happened?" He's stopped frowning, but his face has that paternal look that she loves yet drives her a little crazy. She likes how safe she feels with Red but hates the idea that he might feel like he needs to save her. Her first impulse is to waive it off. Aw, it's nothing. But she knows Red will hear about it some other way and then possibly be upset with her for not fessing up.

"Some Neuro chick thought I was messing with her date and yanked my earring out!" She glances down at their feet. "I was trying to find it, it happened somewhere around here."

Red snorts, "Ooo, I don't think you're gonna have any luck with that. Besides, I don't think you *want* to find it off this nasty floor." He looks around his feet, just the same. Then he looks up and leans in. "So did you get her back?"

Carla shakes her head. "No... I just wanted to stop the

bleeding and get the hell away from her craziness! And, you know, equalize...!" She holds her hands up to show her balance, now that she's done a few lines. She smiles nervously. She knows that Red grasps how much speed she does, more or less. She also knows he's a sometimes-straight edge/sometimes partaker, mostly because he doesn't have a lot of money these days, but sometimes because he just wants to have a clear head. Either way, he doesn't judge.

She can feel the speed coursing through her body, causing her to rock back and forth slightly to its chemical beat. She bites her lower lip and holds it there, reflecting. "Mmm, I think I should head home! I don't want to see her again, and I should clean my ear up better!" She leans around Red to see the stage. "And I really kind of just wanted to find you." She pushes her lower lip into a mock pout, and gazes up at Red like one of those black velvet paintings of doe-eyed, hungry children.

Red looks over at the stage, where Jello Biafra is heckling the crowd, egging them on to fight the power, get politically right, do more crazy shit. He loves this band, their political intellect and 'fuck you' in the face of everything 'the man' holds sacred. But he also loves this girl, and he worries about her sometimes. He sighs.

"Huh, you heading home?"

Carla nods immediately. Yes, hoping he'll at least see her out. Red looks back at the band one more time. Fuck it. There will be other shows. There's only one Carla.

"Well, let me walk you home then. I'm not trusting the streets so much these days." He's referring to that little street kid, Jen. She'd been choked to death and her body left in a dumpster. He would *hate* to think of that happening to Carla. Red raises his eyebrows and nods back towards the entrance of the club. "You ready?"

Carla sweeps her gaze over the floor around them once more. Nope, that cross is gone. Give it up and go home, where it's clean, and quiet, and smells good. She looks up into Red's blue eyes, though they seem grey-ish in the dim light of the club. "Yeah, I'm ready. Thanks," she starts to touch her earlobe, then thinks better of it. "It's not bleeding again, is it?"

Red leans in, gets a whiff of Carla's bright clean, almost bleach-soapy smell. "Nope, you're good." He sweeps his arm towards the exit. Carla just smiles - that doesn't hurt! And leads the way.

Outside, they consider the night. Creeping fog has dropped tendrils along the street and up and down the hill from the Mab. Carla can feel her hair instantly moisten in the soft drizzle of ground-captured dew. A handful of punks gather against the building, beneath the couple of awnings over the entrance to the Mab and the theater next door, smoking and colluding about whatever it is they have going on.

Carla wraps her arms around her thin body and takes a step towards City Lights Booksellers and Grant Street. Red shrugs his leather off, and slips it, heavy and huge, over Carla's slight shoulders. She thanks him with a fleeting smile and that warm glance- even if only one of them is high, they connect- and they make their way up the street, saying 'hey' to the punks they pass.

As they reach the corner of Broadway and Grant, Carla looks back at the club and Carol Doda's brightly lit neon boobs across the street. She looks up at Red and says, "Sorry about making you leave the show." He glances back at the scene she's referring to, "Yeah... Mabuhay Nights. There will be others. So tell me why you were looking for me. What's going on?"

As they turn back to Grant and the long hill climb towards Carla's little pad, she asks him about Jen and Shelly. She leans into him while he tells her what he knows. She burrows into the scent of Red in his leather jacket. He shoves his hands into the front pockets of his jeans and shares what he thinks is starting to happen in their City. And maybe this isn't just another Mabuhay Night.

About the author

Photo by Paula Batzella

Ruby grew up in the foothills of Northern CA and the West Texas flatlands, riding horses in the back woods near Folsom Prison, and singing with family on the back porch. She attended SDSU at fifteen- studying electrical engineering and drama- then stumbled into life on the streets of San Francisco, enchanted by all the grime and glitz, the drugs and wild nights, even the discordance and insanity of life as a punk in those early days.

Moving on, Ruby co-founded the North Coast California Earth First! in Arcata, CA while attending Humboldt State, and fished across Alaskan waters. Eventually, she moved to Seattle, WA where she opened a series of restaurants, then transitioned from restaurateur to singer/songwriter when she started the roots-rockabilly band Ruby Dee and the Snakehandlers in 2002. Thrice Grammy-considered, they tour the world and produce award-winning records.

In 2023, Ruby wrote Bag of Tricks after reconnecting with old punk friends and reminiscing about those lost years. Most of what she wrote came from events that really occurred, though Ruby took liberties and changed some details because she could.

TEN POETS
VOLUME ONE

MARTIN APPLEBY
DAWN VINCENT
JAMES DOMESTIC
AMY WRAGG
LEON THE POET
MARY FUCKING POPPINS
RICCI READ
RICKY FROST
TONKABELL
JACKIE MONTAGUE

Ten Poets (Volume One)
by Martin Appleby, Dawn Vincent, James Domestic, Amy Wragg, Leon The
Poet, Mary Fucking Poppins, Ricci Read, Ricky Frost, Tonkabell, Jackie
Montague.

The first in a series of books showcasing poets of all stripes and intended to
act as a primer to check out their other work and/or book them to perform
in your city, town, or village.

Poetry is arguably in (another) period of renaissance right now – everyone
and their dog is a poet; just check out Instagram or TikTok – but there's
plenty of really terrible poetry around, as there always has been. We don't
want that stuff; we want the diamonds that sparkle in the dirt, those that
are using poetry to connect with audiences, to say something about the
human condition, to make people think, reflect, and maybe even laugh like
drains (poetry on some level is entertainment, and only an inveterate snob
would say otherwise).

For some of the poets that feature in this collection, this is their first
published work. For others, these poems sit alongside their other books,
contributions to literary magazines etc. It doesn't matter; they're all here in
one place and demanding your attention, so dive in and give them some!

Available at www.earthislandbooks.com

E.D. Evans is a lifelong poet. Having spent time in both London and New York during Punk's original heyday in the late '70s and early '80s, Evans has always comfortably floated between those two worlds. She became deeply entrenched in New York's East Village art scene that was so pervasive in the 1980s/90s, spending years performing spoken word poetry at venues such as The Nuyorican Poets Café, Brownies, and The Knitting Factory. Her Instagram handle, @originalpunkster11 says it all.

"I've always liked to tell dark stories that rhyme, so hopefully my words translate into the ethos and audience for which it is intended. What a lot of young Punks today may not realize is that even back in the day, Punk was always about acceptance and inclusion. We were what we were—basically a bunch of creative misfits looking for our tribe, with a great soundtrack to boot. And when we found each other, it was a glorious thing."

Evans currently features her spoken word on social media platforms, and is collaborating with an array of visual artists and musicians to bring her poetry to life. She lives in the Sonoran Desert with parrots, a blind cat, lots of backyard lizards, and a madly talented multi-instrumentalist.

"...And to all our spokespeople who have passed, Rest in Punk. You influenced generations to come, and I, for one, will always be grateful."

available from
EARTH ISLAND BOOKS
WISDOM OF THE PUNK BUDDHA
www.earthislandbooks.com